Public Relations and Online Engagement

As media continues to evolve, social media has become even more integral to public relations activities, presenting new opportunities and challenges for practitioners. Relationships between publics and organizations continue to be first and foremost, but the process and possibilities for mutually beneficial relationships are being rewritten in situ.

This volume aims to explore and understand highly engaged publics in a variety of social media contexts and across networks. The hope is the expansion and extension of public relations theories and models in this book helps move the discipline forward to keep up with the practice and the media environment. Contributors analyzed a range of organizations and industries, including corporate, entertainment, government, and political movements, to consider how public relations practitioners can facilitate ethical and effective communication between parties. A consistent thread was the need for organizations and practitioners to better understand the diverse backgrounds of publics, including age, ethnicity, gender, and sexual orientation, beyond surface-level demographic stereotypes and assumptions.

This book will be of interest to researchers, academics, and students in the field of public relations and communication, especially those with a particular interest in online engagement and social media as a PR tool.

Amber L. Hutchins, Ph.D., is Associate Professor of Communication at the School of Media and Communication at Kennesaw State University in Kennesaw, Georgia.

Natalie T. J. Tindall, Ph.D., serves as Department Chair and is Professor in the Department of Communication and Media at Lamar University.

Routledge Insights in Public Relations Research

The field of PR research has grown exponentially in recent years and academics at all career levels are seeking authoritative publication opportunities for their scholarship. **Routledge Insights in Public Relations Research** is a new program of short-form book publications, presenting key topics across the discipline and their foundation in research. This series will provide a forward-facing global forum for new and emerging research topics which critically evaluate contemporary PR thinking and practice.

This format is particularly effective for introducing new scholarship reflecting the diverse range of research approaches and topics in the field. It is particularly effective for:

- Overview of an emerging area or "hot topic".
- In-depth case-study.
- Tailored research-based information for a practitioner readership.
- Update of a research paper to reflect new findings or wider perspectives.
- Exploration of analytical or theoretical innovations.
- Topical response to current affairs or policy debates.

Authors from practice and the academy will be able to quickly pass on their thinking and findings to fellow PR scholars, researchers, MA and PhD students and informed practitioners.

Public Relations and Sustainable Citizenship
Representing the Unrepresented
Debashish Munshi and Priya Kurian

Public Relations and Online Engagement
Audiences, Fandom and Influencers
Edited by Amber L. Hutchins and Natalie T. J. Tindall

For more information about this series, please visit: www.routledge.com/
Routledge-Insights-in-Public-Relations-Research/book-series/RIPRR

Public Relations and Online Engagement

Audiences, Fandom and Influencers

**Edited by Amber L. Hutchins
and Natalie T. J. Tindall**

Routledge
Taylor & Francis Group

LONDON AND NEW YORK

First published 2021
by Routledge
2 Park Square, Milton Park, Abingdon, Oxon OX14 4RN

and by Routledge
605 Third Avenue, New York, NY 10158

Routledge is an imprint of the Taylor & Francis Group, an informa business

British Library Cataloguing-in-Publication Data
A catalogue record for this book is available from the British Library

Library of Congress Cataloging-in-Publication Data
Names: Hutchins, Amber, editor. | Tindall, Natalie T. J., 1978– editor.
Title: Public relations and online engagement : audiences, fandom and influencers / edited by Amber L. Hutchins, Ph.D. and Natalie T. J. Tindall, Ph.D.
Description: Abingdon, Oxon ; New York : Routledge, 2021. | Series: Routledge insights in public relations research | Includes bibliographical references and index.
Identifiers: LCCN 2021012817 (print) | LCCN 2021012818 (ebook)
Subjects: LCSH: Internet in public relations. | Social media. | Public relations.
Classification: LCC HD59 .P78436 2021 (print) | LCC HD59 (ebook) | DDC 659.20285/4678—dc23
LC record available at https://lccn.loc.gov/2021012817
LC ebook record available at https://lccn.loc.gov/2021012818

ISBN: 978-0-367-34675-1 (hbk)
ISBN: 978-1-032-07325-5 (pbk)
ISBN: 978-0-429-32709-4 (ebk)

DOI: 10.4324/9780429327094

Typeset in Times New Roman
by Apex CoVantage, LLC

Contents

Contributors

Editors

Amber L. Hutchins, Ph.D., is Associate Professor of Communication at the School of Media and Communication at Kennesaw State University in Kennesaw, Georgia. Dr. Hutchins's work extends beyond academia to previous positions in health care, entertainment, and corporate public relations. She has also served as a social media consultant for government and nonprofit organizations. Her research interests include public relations ethics, social media for strategic communication, and fandom.

Natalie T. J. Tindall, Ph.D., serves as Department Chair and is Professor in the Department of Communication and Media at Lamar University. Her research focuses on diversity in organizations, specifically the public relations function, and the situational theory of publics and intersectionality.

Contributors

Mélanie Bourdaa, Ph.D., is Associate Professor at the University of Bordeaux.

Kelli S. Burns, Ph.D., is Associate Professor at the University of South Florida.

Candice Edrington, Ph.D, is Assistant Professor at High Point University.

Ashley Hinck, Ph.D., is Associate Professor at Xavier University.

Leslie Rasmussen, Ph.D., is Associate Professor at Xavier University.

Kathleen Stansberry, Ph.D., is Assistant Professor at Elon University.

Jessalynn Strauss, Ph.D., is Assistant Professor at Elon University.

Kylie P. Torres, M.A., is Instructor at Kennesaw State University.

Elaine Venter, Ph.D., is Assistant Professor at Colorado Mesa University.

Introduction

Amber L. Hutchins

Our previous book, *Public Relations and Participatory Culture: Fandom, Social Media and Community Engagement*, explored how publics are changing in the social media era. We reconsidered traditional categories of publics, created in the context of traditional pre-Internet media, in order to address new behaviors and expectations of individuals who are immersed in participatory culture online. We examined the behaviors of highly engaged publics who create as well as consume content. We also examined online communities and social media networks that encourage and facilitate increased strength of ties between publics, as well as between publics and organizations. While traditional public relations research also considers marketing and business theories, models, and concepts to understand audiences and consumer behavior, we considered highly engaged publics in the context of fan studies and media studies, as many of the behaviors, communities, and relationships we sought to understand resembled those more closely associated with entertainment. As such, the terms *brandfans*, *fanpublics*, and *charged publics* were explored, developed, and created in our book to expand the discourse about publics in both scholarly research and practice of public relations. Since publication, additional examples of highly engaged publics and communities have emerged, as well as new social media platforms, practices, environmental factors and societal situations, and this collection of chapters aims to add perspective and new direction for further study.

This volume aims to continue to explore and understand highly engaged publics in a variety of social media contexts and across networks. As media continues to evolve, social media has become even more integral to public relations activities, presenting new opportunities and challenges for practitioners. Relationships between publics and organizations continue to be first and foremost, but the process and possibilities for mutually beneficial relationships are being rewritten in situ. We hope the expansion and extension

DOI: 10.4324/9780429327094-1

of public relations theories and models in this book helps move the discipline forward to keep up with the practice and the media environment.

Our contributors analyzed a range of organizations and industries, including corporate, entertainment, government, and political movements, to consider how public relations practitioners can facilitate ethical and effective communication between parties. A consistent thread was the need for organizations and practitioners to better understand the diverse backgrounds of publics, including age, ethnicity, gender, and sexual orientation, beyond surface-level demographic stereotypes and assumptions. By immersing ourselves in the communities we communicate with, practitioners and scholars can develop equitable relationships with highly engaged publics.

It is important to note that the chapters in this text were researched and written both before and during the 2020 COVID-19 global pandemic, the protests after the killing of George Floyd, and the 2020 U.S. elections. Included in this book are chapters by Edrington, Hinck and Rasmussen, and Torres, which shed light on these situations from a professional communication perspective. But we also observed that chapters written before the pandemic explored situations, theory, behaviors, and practices that have been amplified during quarantine and lockdown situations, as publics look for connection and meaning in social media. Together, all of the chapters included in this book provide timely and valuable insights as practitioners and scholars look forward and to the future.

1 From slacktivism to activism

Rihanna and Fenty brands "pull up"

Candice Edrington

Introduction

The examination of how activist organizations and advocacy groups intersect with public relations has been a particular area of focus for many scholars in recent years (Ciszek, 2015; Edrington & Lee, 2018; Choi, Overton, & McKeever, 2018). Social movements, more specifically, have piqued much interest as they have made great strides in their communication, heightened visibility, narrative creation and development, and collective mobilization across the digital media (Edrington & Gallagher, 2019). Building and maintaining a strong member base is not the only relationships that social movements can benefit from. Activating support from organizations with similar goals may also be beneficial. Having organizations and celebrities participate in social media campaigns designed to bring awareness to movement efforts, especially when they have a "navy" behind them, is one good way to build and activate that support. Social media platforms have made aiding in the visibility and narrative development of social movements a bit easier while also providing nontraditional media avenues for organizations and their leadership to advocate for or against issues in a more informal way. Given the political polarization in America, organizations are expected to take a stance on social-political issues now more than ever. In this chapter, I explore how Rihanna and her Fenty brands used Instagram to transition from the performative act of just "posting" to the practical task of "pulling up" during the most recent Black Lives Matter (BLM) movement social media campaigns following the deaths of Ahmaud Arbery, Breonna Taylor, and George Floyd.

Black lives matter

Appearing on social media after the acquittal of George Zimmerman for the murder of unarmed teenager Trayvon Martin, the three words "black

DOI: 10.4324/9780429327094-2

lives matter," written by BLM co-founder Patrisse Cullors, concluded a love letter to Black people authored by Alicia Garza. Emerging once again on Twitter after the shooting death of unarmed African American teenager Michael Brown Jr. in 2014, the phrase "black lives matter" gained momentum and became a hashtag movement, quickly initiating the long overdue and often uncomfortable conversation about racial inequality in America. Writers Anderson and Hitlin (2016) posited "the #blacklivesmatter hashtag appeared an average of 58,747 times per day in the roughly three weeks following Brown's death" (Anderson & Hitlin, 2016, para. 10). Through the use of the hashtag #BlackLivesMatter, people locally, nationally, and globally were able to view the very graphic image of the slain teen's body lying in the street of Ferguson as well as the discourse that circulated with it. This hashtag increased the visibility of the social injustices faced by African Americans for those who were otherwise naïve, similar to the 1991 video of Rodney King in South Central L.A. Because of this, they were able to witness and join the conversation with others.

#BlackLivesMatter quickly moved from online participation to collective mobilization. Over the course of a few months, more reports of killings of African Americans by White law enforcement officers flooded the media. After the enormous response from other activists, Garza and her two friends (Cullors and Tometi) decided to organize the idea of #BlackLivesMatter into an official organization. #BlackLivesMatter transformed into the Black Lives Matter movement with the creation of an official website (Edrington, 2020).

With hopes of ending police brutality against African American people, BLM's strength rested on the new opportunities provided by social media platforms. These platforms allowed users to share their experiences regarding police brutality, racism, and discrimination, to connect with others across the globe with whom they may have identified, to share resources regarding movement efforts such as protests, to circulate pictures and videos of such instances, and to amplify the voices of marginalized communities.

The endeavors to eradicate White supremacy, end police brutality against Black bodies, and bring about social justice did not end after Brown's 2014 death. In fact, they had only just begun. Unfortunately, people across the globe continued to witness acts of brutality, discrimination, and injustice inflicted upon unarmed Black people as videos of police shootings continued to be released and circulated. Seemingly, there was another name behind a hashtag on social media that pushed BLM back into the public sphere every year. Social media users would repost images of the victims, voice their frustrations once again, and even protest. Some brands also voiced their support for BLM and efforts toward racial equality and justice. In 2020, however, something was different.

#BlackoutTuesday

As the world paused due to the global pandemic, more and more people began to pay attention to the BLM movement and understand its agenda. With stay-at-home orders in place, we were all constantly tuned in to news sources for the latest on the coronavirus. What we didn't expect, however, was exposure to another pandemic, racial injustice. First, there was the shooting death of Ahmaud Arbery in February. While Arbery, unarmed, wasn't killed by an active police officer, the video that circulated months (in May) after his murder showed him being gunned down by two white men as he jogged through his neighborhood. In March, the news of Breonna Taylor's murder surfaced and began to go viral on social media. Although there was no footage of the shooting released, the reports of Taylor, an unarmed Black woman, being murdered by cops as she slept due to a "no knock" warrant created an uproar on social media. The murder of George Floyd in May pushed Americans over the edge. Emotions were at an all-time high as we watched the eight minute and 46 second video of a white officer kneeling on Floyd's neck, ultimately resulting in his death. According to Alex Altman (2020), writer for *Time*, "the timing and cruelty of Floyd's death, captured in a horrific video, spurred, a national uprising" (Altman, 2020, para. 3). Unlike anything that has ever happened before, Floyd's death awakened a racial reckoning.

In a matter of four months, the murders of three unarmed Black people were highly publicized. Several social media campaigns were created to call for justice such as #IRunWithMaud, #JusticeForBreonna, and #JusticeforGeorge. Another social media campaign, #BlackoutTuesday, generated a lot of participation. Stemming from #TheShowMustBePaused initiative created by two Black women music industry executives, Jamila Thomas and Brianna Agyemang, the #BlackoutTuesday social media campaign served as a pledge to disconnect from business as usual and to reconnect with the community. The purpose of this campaign was to show support and solidarity for the Black community. On June 2, black squares flooded social media platforms followed by the caption #BlackoutTuesday. On that Tuesday, black squares captioned with #BlackoutTuesday flooded social media, mainly Instagram. Although the campaign was great in that it added to the narrative of racial inequality, it was met with resounding mixed reviews. Before noon, "more than 14.6 million Instagram posts used the hashtag #BlackoutTuesday" according to *CNBC* writers Jessica Bursztynsky and Sarah Whitten (2020) (Bursztynsky & Whitten, 2020, para. 2). The collective participation in this effort ranged from those inside and outside of the music industry, and everyday citizens. Beyond the hashtags and black squares, record labels and other companies used the day to hold town-hall meetings, donate money, and plan future action. Fenty Beauty founder Rihanna made headlines with her participation in #BlackoutTuesday.

Rihanna and Fenty "pull up"

Through her intentional celebration of diversity in her beauty and fashion brands, Rihanna "continues to disrupt the status quo" (Saini, 2018, para. 6). As a longtime philanthropist and advocate for social justice, Rihanna often uses her social media platforms to bring about awareness to certain issues. In 2019, she turned down the opportunity to perform at the Super Bowl halftime show in solidarity with Colin Kaepernick. Unsurprisingly, singer-songwriter and beauty mogul Rihanna participated in #BlackoutTuesday. Continuing to advocate on behalf of the Black Lives Matter movement, Rihanna posted messages of support for the #BlackoutTuesday campaign on her personal Instagram page @badgalriri and on all three of her Fenty brand Instagram pages (@fenty, @fentybeauty, and @savagexfenty). In addition to posting the black square and messages of support, Rihanna paused all operations of her three brands for the day.

Fenty

Founded in 2019 with Moët Hennessy Louis Vuitton (LVMH), Fenty is a fashion brand that "values freedom, defiance, and culture" (Fenty, 2020). In addition to the image of a black square, Fenty posted another image with this caption:

> Fenty as a brand was created to elevate beauty, power, and freedom! At this very moment racists are attempting to rip those values away from black people and we will NOT stand by and let that happen. We are too powerful, creative, and resilient. In support of the black community, we will be donating funds to Color of Change and Movement for Black Lives. We ask you to speak up, stand up, and pull up against racism and discrimination in all forms.
>
> —@fenty

This post generated over 45,000 likes and 333 comments at the time of this writing. Another post on the Fenty Instagram page highlighted the pausing of operations:

> We are not staying silent and we are not standing by. The fight against racial inequality, injustice, and straight up racism doesn't stop with financial donations and words of support. In solidarity with the Black community, our employees, our friends, our families, and our colleagues

across the industries we are proud to take part in #BlackoutTuesday. Fenty will NOT be conducting any business on Tuesday, June 2 globally. This is not a day off. This is a day to reflect and find ways to make real change. This is a day to #PullUp #BlackoutTuesday.

—@fenty

At the time of this writing, this post generated over 34,000 likes with 254 comments.

Fenty Beauty

Created in 2017, Fenty Beauty is a cosmetic brand that "was created with promise of inclusion for all women" (Fenty Beauty, 2020). On June 2nd, Fenty Beauty posted a black square with the same caption as the Fenty Instagram account. The only difference was the addition of the phrase Black Lives Matter which was originally posted as a hashtag. The post was edited after receiving backlash for combining the two hashtags which had a negative impact on information sharing regarding the movement. On this particular post, there were over 141,000 likes and 1,081 comments. To further highlight their acts of solidarity and activism, Fenty Beauty shared an image on June 4 announcing partnership with the Clara Lionel Foundation in support of the NAACP Legal Defense Fund.

Savage X Fenty – lingerie brand

Also created in 2017, Savage X Fenty is a lingerie line created by Rihanna to "celebrate fearlessness, confidence, and inclusivity" (Savage X Fenty, 2020). Similar to the other two Fenty brands, a black square was posted on the official Instagram account with the same caption as the others. However, this particular image was posted on June 1 and referenced the actions that would be taken on June 2. With over 58,000 likes and 387 comments, the words Black Lives Matter were not attached to this post. Savage X Fenty also partnered with the Clara Lionel Foundation to donate funds for Black Lives Matter of Greater New York and the Bail Project.

The comments under all of these posts display common themes of support, hashtag flooding, and #pullupforchange. The comments that are closely associated with the theme of support reaffirm their love for Rihanna and declare that they will continue to support her and the brand. An overwhelming number of comments provide insight into how the use of #BLM and #BlackoutTuesday together creates hashtag flooding and asks that the former hashtag be removed. Lastly, several comments asked the founder to join the #pullupforchange challenge. This Instagram challenge asks brands who voice their support for the Black Lives Matter movement and Black community to release the diversity numbers of their employees. While Fenty Beauty did address the hashtag flooding by removing the hashtag from the phrase Black Lives Matter, none of the brands have yet produced a report of their employee diversity.

Conclusion

On June 2, 2020, music industry executives launched the #BlackoutTuesday social media campaign in support of the Black Lives Matter movement and the Black community. The purpose of this initiative was to pause normal activity and business operations for the day and reconnect with the community in some manner. Although well intentioned, many Instagram users and activists noted that the use of #BlackoutTuesday and #BlackLivesMatter coupled together in a caption under the black square had negative repercussions. According to James Vincent (2020), writer for *The Verge*, the combining of these hashtags "obscured a channel that's being used to share vital information about protests, organization donations, and document police violence" (Vincent, 2020, para. 1). Additionally, some viewed the simple act of posting a black square on social media platforms as a form of slacktivism, "the act of passively supporting causes in order to tap into the satisfaction that accompanies philanthropy without having to do the heavy-lifting" (Davis, 2011, para. 9).

Typically framed negatively as it relates to concretely helping social justice efforts, there are some advantages to slacktivism. When organizations or celebrities participate in slacktivism, it can expose new audiences to the cause, as shown in the case of Rihanna and the Fenty brand. Given that all three of Fenty's brands support inclusivity and culture, it is not surprising that they would be very active and vocal regarding the recent killings of unarmed Black people that have materialized into global uprisings. As champions of diversity and inclusion since their inception, Fenty and its other brand components are authentically millennial in their message strategies and positioning. Based on previous branding initiatives, it is obvious that the voices in the room making the front-facing decisions are diverse; it becomes apparent in their responses to #BlackoutTuesday.

As the only brand housed under LVMH to participate in #BlackoutTuesday, the case of Rihanna and the Fenty brand is unique. By showing support and solidarity with both the Black community and the Black Lives Matter movement, Fenty chose to remain authentic in their mission for diversity and inclusion. Despite the potential polarization of its stakeholders, Rihanna and the Fenty brand placed their customers' needs at the center of their efforts instead of choosing to focus on profits. For public relations practitioners, this case study boasts the importance of knowing your audience and engaging accordingly. Through an analysis of the comments under all Fenty brand entities' posts, it becomes apparent that their #Blackout-Tuesday efforts were appreciated. Most customers reiterated their love and support of both Rihanna and the brands, while others vowed to become new supporters/customers. For social movement organizers, this case study illuminates how support from organizations and celebrities with similar agendas can aide in the narrative and help increase the visibility of the movement's agenda through message sharing and collective mobilization.

References

Altman, A. (2020, June 4). *Why the killing of George Floyd sparked an American uprising.* Retrieved from https://time.com/5847967/george-floyd-protests-trump/

Anderson, M., & Hitlin, P. (2016, August 15). *The hashtag #BlackLivesMatter emerges: Social activism on Twitter.* Retrieved from www.pewinternet.org/2016/08/15/the-hashtag-blacklivesmatter-emerges-social-activism-on-twitter/

Bursztynsky, J., & Whitten, S. (2020, June 2). *Instagram users flood the app with millions of Blackout Tuesday posts.* Retrieved from www.cnbc.com/2020/06/02/instagram-users-flood-the-app-with-millions-of-blackout-tuesday-posts.html

Choi, M., Overton, H., & McKeever, R. (2018). When organizational advocacy and public advocacy intersect in csr: Examining stage of partnership and activism in csr partnerships. *Journal of Public Interest Communications, 2*(2), 264–288.

Ciszek, E. (2015). Bridging the gap: Mapping the relationship between activism and public relations. *Public Relations Review, 41*(4), 447–455.

Davis, J. (2011, October 27). *Cause marketing: Moving beyond corporate slacktivism* [Web blog post]. Retrieved from http://evidencebasedmarketing.net/cause-marketing-moving-beyond-corporate-slacktivism

Edrington, C. (2020). *Identification and relationships: How social movements use and articulate identification across digital platforms to build relationships* [Doctoral dissertation, North Carolina State University]. Retrieved from https://repository.lib.ncsu.edu/bitstream/handle/1840.20/37347/etd.pdf?sequence=1&isAllowed=y

Edrington, C., & Gallagher, V. (2019). Race and visibility: How and why images of Black lives matter. *Visual Communication Quarterly, 26*(4), 195–207.

Edrington, C., & Lee, N. (2018). Tweeting a social movement: Black lives matter and its use of Twitter to share information, build community, and promote action. *The Journal of Public Interest Communications, 2*(2), 289. doi:10.32473/jpic.v2.i2.p289

Fenty. (2020). *About us.* Retrieved from www.fenty.com/us/en/home

Fenty [@fenty]. (n.d.). *Posts* [Instagram profile]. Retrieved July 10, 2020 from www.instagram.com/fenty/

Fenty Beauty. (2020). *About us.* Retrieved from www.fentybeauty.com/about-fenty

Fenty Beauty [@fentybeauty]. (n.d.). *Posts* [Instagram profile]. Retrieved July 10, 2020 from www.instagram.com/fentybeauty/

Rihanna [@badgalriri]. (n.d.). *Posts* [Instagram profile]. Retrieved July 10, 2020 from www.instagram.com/badgalriri/

Saini, N. (2018, August 14). How beauty disruptors are changing the cosmetic and skincare industry. Retrieved from www.prestigeonline.com/sg/beauty-wellness/beauty-disruptors-changing-cosmetic-skincare-industry/

Savage X Fenty. (2020). *About us*. Retrieved from www.savagex.com

Savage X Fenty [@savagexfenty]. (n.d.). *Posts* [Instagram profile]. Retrieved July 10, 2020 from www.instagram.com/savagexfenty/

Vincent, J. (2020, June 2). *Blackout Tuesday posts are drowning out vital information shared under the BLM hashtag*. Retrieved from www.theverge.com/2020/6/2/21277852/blackout-tuesday-posts-hiding-information-blm-black-lives-matter-hashtag

2 Saving Wynonna Earp

The power of fandom

Mélanie Bourdaa

Among the many fans' activities, some can be at the intersection of cultural, social, and political participation and involve an increased level of civic engagement, especially among young fans who use media platforms and especially social networks as a platform.[1]

This chapter will analyze the correlation between fannish activities and social engagement in the form of lobbying to better understand how fans draw on their collective identity to mobilize and recruit and how the relationship between fans and showrunners and actors of TV shows could be redefined.

I will also highlight the importance of new technologies to open up possibilities for activist fans. When they fight to save their series, fans create a relevant organization in their community. But above all, they prove that they understand the economic stakes of the media ecosystem to foil them or to reclaim them.

I will present *Wynonna Earp* (Syfy, 2016-present) as a case study because the #fightforwynonna hashtag campaign is the perfect example of the "power of fandom" when it comes to supporting the cast and crew of a TV show. This genre series, which combines Western and fantasy, stars Melanie Scrofano as Wynonna Earp, fictional descendant of the famous Wyatt Earp, struggling with ghosts and demons who fight to destroy the Earp family. As both the heir and the chosen one, she alone can kill and send them back to hell with a special pistol called Peacemaker. This series is an adaptation by showrunner Emily Andras of Beau Smith's comic book for IDW Publishing.

As entertainment reporter Maureen Ryan pointed out in *The New York Times* on the eve of the first episode of Season 3, "*Wynonna Earp* demonstrates how a distinctive premise, a passionate fanbase and a creative team that respects and nurtures that enthusiasm can help an under-the-radar show flourish in a TV landscape that is tough even on acclaimed shows" (Ryan, 2018).

DOI: 10.4324/9780429327094-3

On a methodological point, I posted an online questionnaire to know what draws fans to the show and what makes the fandom important for them. Via Twitter, I collected the hashtag #fightforwynonna, which fans created to lead the campaign. I could thus measure fans' engagement with the campaign, how they organized themselves, and which content they posted.

A brief history of the "Save Our Show" campaigns

The first manifestation of fans' social engagement translates into increased lobbying to save their favorite television series. But it turns out that the "Save Our Show" campaigns demonstrate, above all, an evolution of the negotiations between the audiences and the channels or the sponsors of the series. Showrunners have also understood the importance of the support they can get from communities to put pressure on networks.

Two recent examples illustrate this point. The showrunners of the time-travel series, *Timeless* (NBC, 2017–2019), asked their fan base to help save the series from cancellation. Eric Kripke, the showrunner, posted a letter asking for fans' support before the last episodes aired, knowing full well that the fans would mobilize. Despite a strong and loyal fan community, the audiences were not strong enough to avoid a cancellation from the network after its first season, but as Sharon Marie Ross notes:

> the fact that industry professionals seem to be seeking tele-participation and extension of the TV suggests that the tele-participating viewer is becoming a prototype – and real or imagined, the *perception* of the social audience is often as important as the actuality of the social audience when it comes to what the industry will offer.
>
> (Ross, 2008, p. 15)

The relationship between fans and showrunners in this context is a relationship of mutual help because the series, especially when on a network, cannot continue to exist without the support of a particularly active and committed audience. The showrunners and the fate of the series are in the hands of this specific audience, thus reversing the unilateral and descending power relations that existed until then between production and reception.

Social networks represent a privileged platform that fans use to carry out their actions and give them a certain visibility and echo in the public sphere. The organization is set up within the fan community itself, the rules of the game are enacted by fans themselves, but the permeability and porosity of social networks allow them to make their actions visible and known.

Even if social networks amplify the voice of the fans, the "Save Our Show" campaigns existed well before the Internet and had the same characteristics as today: a collective and collaborative organization, a common desire to defend the series and advocate for them. It is then interesting to go back to a small historical overview of the most relevant campaigns.

The first major campaign took place in 1968 around the original *Star Trek* TV show, at a time when fan communities were meeting in conventions dedicated to science fiction and genre shows, physical places where they could discuss face to face and share fanzines. After the lack of audiences during the second season and the cancellation threats by the network, fans mobilized through fanzines where they published advice and guidelines to follow as a group. They sent a hundred and fifteen thousand letters to support the show to the network. In the end, the network aired a third season. Some other famous campaigns include Cagney and Lacy, Hill Street Blues, or Beauty and the Beast for example (Guerrero-Pico, 2017).

Another campaign was forged around *Veronica Mars* (UPN-The CW, 2004–2008). After the announcement of the cancellation at the end of the third season, fans organized themselves in discussion forums dedicated to the series, including the website *Television Without Pity*, to try and save it. After some debates on how best to operate, they decided together to send a million Mars chocolate bars to the WB network to show that there was an active audience ready to defend and watch the series. This first attempt was a failure since the show wasn't renewed for a fourth season at the time. However, Rob Thomas, the showrunner, and Kristen Bell, the lead actress, launched a "Kickstarter" crowdfunding campaign in 2013 and asked for fans' donations to fund a *Veronica Mars* movie. This fundraising raised more than $ 2 million in less than 12 hours, exceeding the expectations of the actress and producer. Clearly, they both relied on the emotional, intellectual, and economic investment of fans to revive the series, and play on the desire of fans to have a "real" ending, to reap sufficient funding to produce a movie. In this context, fans become co-producers, in the economic and literal sense of the term, of the *Veronica Mars* movie. We are beyond the *gift-economy*, which advocates noncommercial exchanges between fans. Here, the fans, in exchange for a co-funding, receive concrete goods and material objects in the form of the film in digital version, t-shirts, posters, and stickers that allow supporters to display their status of fans and their economic contribution. In an article about this specific campaign, Bethan Chin et al. (2014) notes that fans know full well that they give to a big studio, but at the same time, they participate in the construction of a collective project. Indeed, more than funding a studio film (here Warner Bros), fans are more likely to participate in this campaign to fund the creativity of the showrunner who created the series. In this context, Matt Hills talks about affective economy (Hills, 2015) and Suzanne Scott about fan-ancing (Scott, 2015), focusing on the new economy generated by the relationship between production and reception, as well as a moral economy that disrupts the traditional channels of production and dissemination of audiovisual contents.

In these "Save Our Show" campaigns, fans act as lobbyists or advocates. They also play the part of public relations practitioners, in the sense that they put together an action and make it visible, as well as the show, to the public. Their collective organization shows a good understanding of their "strike force." But above all, today, they use social networks as a platform for meeting up, hiring, and building up actions in the public sphere to defend their series and try to save them. Finally, fans are aware of the series' production mechanisms and economic issues and do not hesitate to appropriate and divert them to achieve their goals. Thus, rather than viewing fans as pure consumers and passive audiences, these campaigns reflect their activity, their collective organization, and their understanding of the current media ecosystem.

"It starts at the top": inclusion and interactions between fans and the cast and crew

As I mentioned before, *Wynonna Earp* attracts a loyal fan base, mostly women who call themselves Earpers. The collective identity of the *Wynonna Earp* fan community begins with the choice of a name that allows members to self-identify as fans of the show and identify themselves in the digital world. An Earper is a fan of the Syfy show *Wynonna Earp*. The Earper Fandom is known for their acceptance among/love for other Earpers, as well as their extreme, over-the-top obsessing over the show's cast and popular LGBTQA+ couple known to fans as "WayHaught." What is the most important for this "famdom" (family/fandom), as they call their community, is the inclusion of all members. And this inclusion is, according to the responses I collected, an example to follow from what the cast and crew are doing. For questionnaire respondent "Christinedras":

> It starts up with Emily Andras. She shows us the example. Be open, understanding, have compassion. It goes from there to the cast and the team who have the same values. Earpers are inspired by it and apply it to everyday life on social networks or in real life.

Some answers to our questionnaire confirm that fans of the series do not engage in the toxic practices that may be experienced by other fandoms: "Twitter is a terrible place and there are so many things that can depress me . . . The Wynonna Earp Community does nothing on this awful side and that is what qualifies it for me" (respondent 82).

I also asked a question about the many interactions between the cast and crew and the fans in my online questionnaire. And the answers confirmed and reinforced the idea that the team maintains respectful relationships with its fans, which of course motivates them to interact even more and promote the series.

Recurring themes in the Earper "famdom": respect, authenticity, and care

The term *authentic* is interesting in a context of interactions that may seem controlled by the actors and producers of the series, but which, by their content and frequencies, will seem real to the fans. Boyd and Marwick speak of a "performative practice" of celebrities on social media that includes an "ongoing maintenance of a fanbase, performed intimacy, authenticity and access, and construction of a consommable persona" (boyd, Marwick, 2011, p. 140).

In the interactions and exchanges between fans and the crew and cast, a performative practice is played out in which the teams will maintain an affiliation by using the language codes and cultural symbols of the community, thus leading to a connection. This intimacy is enhanced by creating a sense of familiarity with the fans when teams unveil themselves through selfies or behind-the-scenes pictures for example.

It is also interesting to note that there was a gender issue in this specific campaign. Fans of Wynonna Earp are mostly women and mostly part of the LGBTQA+ community (or ally of the community), and these actions gave a loud voice to this community especially after the return of the *Bury Your Gays Trope*, in which fans spoke out about the trend of LGBTQA+ character deaths, most prominently the debacle following Lexa's death in *The 100* (see Bourdaa, 2018). Women fans and LGBTQA+ fans created their own activist online platform to show that representation matters and that a series could be important enough to make people come together in a common fight.

#fightforWynonna: Earpers at the rescue

In February 2019, fans of the show began to worry because production hadn't started yet (which was unusual compared to the filming of past seasons) and rallied on twitter to voice their concerns. The production was delayed because IDW Publishing, which funded the show, was struggling financially and wasn't able to put money into the show at the time. Meanwhile, Syfy declared it was still committed to air the fourth season as announced at *San Diego Comic Con* the year before. At the times, Emily

Andras gathered fans with an eloquent "don't fuck with my family," suggesting she needed the support of the fandom.

Fans mobilized on social networks, especially Twitter, their digital playground and meeting point, to advocate for the show and give visibility to their concerns and actions. Immediately, the hashtag #fightforWynonna began trending worldwide, showing that fans were ready to fight and have their show back on the screen. They took their actions one step further when they bought more than 80 message billboards in New York City's Times Square to literally show their support to the world. They even dubbed themselves the #billboardcrew and called Times Square "Earp Square," meeting there, taking pictures with posters, taking pictures of the billboards, and posting them online, thus spreading the word and contents in the public sphere. They changed the hashtag to #Win4Wynonna to show that they were confident the outcome would be positive. Emily Andras, Melanie Scrofano (who plays Wynonna), and Tim Rozon (Doc Holliday) also bought billboards to thank fans for their support, reinforcing the friendship and family interactions fans were talking about in my online questionnaire.

What is interesting is how the Earpers organized themselves to bring awareness to their actions and appeal to the producers and broadcasters. First of all, they created and posted guidelines to coordinate their actions[2] and have more impact and more visibility. These guidelines contain advice on how and who to tweet, email, or call, targeting key people in the renewal of the show. They also state that this is a nonaggressive campaign, referring to the inclusiveness of the fandom and the nontoxic practices inside it. Bridget Lisweski, longtime fan of the show and very vocal on social networks, wrote: "Each and everyone of us matter in this fight and it's going to take all of us working together to make it happen."[3] These signs of encouragement are what make the fandom so special for fans; a place where everybody matters and can do what they can for the show and the cast and crew. Fans also documented all their actions,[4] posting weekly recaps with Twitter screencaps and pictures, for newcomers and fans that wanted to follow the evolution of the campaign. That way, they built a case for the fight, proving that their actions made an impact and were not aggressive in any way. They also posted IDW's and Netflix's responses that used their fandom's name in order to show the companies know who they are.

"Save Our Show campaign": new ways of fighting for producers and fans

The "Save Our Show campaigns" are interesting to analyze in order to witness the evolving relationship between producers and fans and how this relationship can lead to social activism. For *Wynonna Earp*, given the constant interactions between the cast and crew and the fans, they thought Emily Andras and the actors were worthy of their support and were an integral part of the famdom, the family they have built for themselves. Seeing the show threatened meant that the family, their safe haven, was also threatened and they gathered to protect it together. It is also interesting to note that there was a gender issue in this specific campaign. As I mentioned before, fans of Wynonna Earp are mostly women and mostly part of the LGBTQA+ community (or ally of the community), and these actions gave a loud voice to this community especially after the return of the *Bury Your Gay Trope*, in which fans spoke out about the trend of LGBTQA+ character deaths, most prominently the debacle following Lexa's death in *The 100* (see Bourdaa, 2018). Women fans and LGBTQA+ fans created their own activist online platform to show that representation matters and that a series could be important to make people come together in a common fight.

Notes

1 A great number of articles have been written on The *Harry Potter Alliance*, for example, and how this organization paves the way for fans to become citizens and politically engaged.
2 https://wynonnaearpfans.com/2019/03/12/fightforwynonna-the-story-so-far/
3 *Ibid.*
4 https://wynonnaearpfans.com/2019/02/22/wynonna-earp-season-4-the-fight-is-on/

References

Bourdaa, M. (2018). May we meet again: Social bonds, activities and identities in the #Clexa fandom. In P. Booth (Ed.), *A companion to media fandom and fan studies* (pp. 385–400). Hoboken, NJ: Wiley-Blackwell.

Boyd, d., & Marwick, A. (2011). To see and be seen: Celebrity practice on twitter. *Convergence: The International Journal of Research in New Media Technologies*, *17*(2), 139–158.

Chin, B., Jones, B., McNutt, M., & Pebler, L. (2014). *Veronica Mars* Kickstarter and crowd funding [dialogue]. In M. Stanfill & M. Condis (Eds.), *Fandom and/ as Labor*. Special issue, *Transformative Works and Cultures* (15). http://dx.doi.org/10.3983/twc.2014.0519

Guerrero-Pico, M. (2017). Fringe, audiences and fan labor: Twitter activism to save a TV Show from cancellation. *International Journal of Communication*, *11*, 2071–2092.

Hills, M. (2015). Veronica Mars, fandom and the affective economics of crowdfunding poachers. *New Media and Society*, *17*(2), 183–197.

Ross, S. M. (2008). *Beyond the box: Television and the internet*. Malden, MA: Blackwell.

Ryan, M. (2018, July 6). A cult's show recipe for success: Whiskey, twitter and complex women. *New York Times*. Retrieved from www.nytimes.com/2018/07/06/arts/television/wynonna-earp-syfy.html

Scott, S. (2015). The moral economy of crowdfunding and the transformative capacity of fan-ancing, *New Media and Society*, *17*(2), 167–182.

3 Learning from the best

A review of community building, audience engagement, and influencer campaigns from the 2019 Cannes Lions

Kelli S. Burns

The Cannes Lions International Festival of Creativity honors the best work in the creative communications industry from the past year. In 2019, the festival included almost 31,000 entries from 89 countries (Cannes Lions, 2019). A review of the entries that made the shortlists in various categories can provide insights into how these campaigns built communities, engaged audiences, and inspired influencers.

One of the specialist Lions tracks for entries and awards is the PR Lions, which recognizes work under categories such as the use of influencers, community building, and user-generated content. Another specialist Lions track is the Social and Influencer Lions, under which are similar categories for community building, influencer marketing, and partnerships. Table 3.1 provides a summary of the categories under these two tracks that relate to influencers, engagement, and community building.

This chapter will explore the following research questions:

1 What tactics do the 2019 Cannes Lions shortlisted campaigns use to build community?
2 What types of co-created and user-generated content is produced in Cannes Lions shortlisted campaigns?
3 Among the entry categories that recognize campaigns with influencers, who are the influencers in Cannes Lions shortlisted campaigns?

These questions will be answered through a qualitative review of the best examples of community building, engagement, and influencer use from the Cannes Lions shortlisted entry videos supplemented with trade publication articles and case studies available on agency websites.

DOI: 10.4324/9780429327094-4

Table 3.1 Cannes Lions Entry Categories under the PR Lions and Social & Influencer Lions Tracks Reviewed for this Study

Track	Category
PR Lions	
	Social Community Building & Management
	Co-creation and User-Generated Content
	Use of Celebrity, Influencers and Key Opinion Leaders
Social & Influencer Lions	
	Community Building and Management
	Innovative Use of Community
	Partnerships
	Innovative Use of Influencers

Community-building tactics

Both the PR Lions and the Social & Influencer Lions tracks recognize work that builds or maintains an online community that increases affinity toward the brand. One commonality of many of the 2019 campaigns is engaging people through a social media hashtag. "Miles for the People" by Grey Brazil addressed the issue of politicians traveling on taxpayer budgets but keeping the airline miles for themselves. The campaign encouraged people to turn to social media using the hashtag #MilesforthePeople to ask politicians to donate miles to various causes.

"The People's Seat," the Gold Lion winner in this category, by Grey London for the United Nations addressed climate change during the UN Climate Change Conference. A physical chair was used to signify that participants could virtually have a seat at the conference through the use of the hashtag #TakeYourSeat.

Another campaign using a hashtag was "The Real Machado de Assis" by Grey Brazil for the Zumbi dos Palmares. The campaign accurately recreated Brazilian writer Machado de Assis's image as a Black man based on historical data and recently discovered photos. The campaign created a conversation around racism with the hashtag #machadodeassisreal and produced an accompanying website with a link to a Change.org petition to get publishers and booksellers to stop printing or selling books with the outdated image.

In another community-building strategy, a stunt involving an influencer was used to drive social media conversation and connected fans through their initial outrage. Uber's campaign "Distracted Goalkeeper" by Tech and Soul focused on the safety issue of distracted driving caused by cell phone use. At the heart of the campaign was a stunt involving Brazilian football goalie Aderbar dos Santos Neto using his phone on the field prior to the game. Fans expressed their outrage about his distraction on social media, and when it was revealed that his behavior was a stunt for a safe-driving campaign, media coverage helped spread the message.

Another community-building stunt was created by Gang London for mental health awareness. The mysterious World Record Egg (@world_record_egg) sought to become the most liked post on Instagram, a goal it accomplished when it surpassed a Kylie Jenner post. An ad on Hulu just after the Super Bowl revealed the egg to have a message about mental health and directed viewers to Mental Health America for a mental health screening.

Community building can also occur in a space where a community already exists, such as on the video game platform Twitch. Grand Prix winner "Keeping Fortnite Fresh" by Wendy's and VMLY&R, noting that burger restaurants on Fortnite featured freezers for storing beef (and Wendy's never uses frozen beef), used a "Wendy" avatar on Fortnite who destroyed burger freezers. On Twitter, they posted a link to send gamers to Twitch to watch Wendy play, and other players joined in the freezer destroying. Prominent Twitch streamers also commented on Wendy's tactics when they saw her in the game.

Finally, community building can tap into an existing public concern. "The Popsicle Elections" by Los Paleteros capitalized on a law in Costa Rica that does not allow political polls to be published up to a week before a presidential election. The ice cream company created two identical ice pop bars with the exception of the color – one for the conservative party and the other for the liberal party. Sales for each store were tracked online and because these were the only poll results available so close to the election, however unscientific, they created significant buzz on social and traditional media.

Co-created and user-generated content

Through an online community, brands may be able to encourage participants to contribute or collaborate with a brand by creating their own content, which will further deepen their connection to the brand. In some campaigns, particularly some discussed above, the content created is at the user's discretion and tends to be mostly tweets and Instagram posts. The campaigns in this section are either more structured in how a user creates content or encourage the creation of something more inspired than tweets. These campaigns were either shortlisted entries for co-created or user-generated content or pulled from other categories from Table 3.1 as being good examples of incorporating user-generated content.

Some campaigns provide participants with content, such as a graphic, to use to co-create content. Wunderman Thompson's campaign "I Love My Balls" for the League Against Cancer focused on cancers affecting men. The campaign flipped the popular "hand heart" upside down and created a colorful graphic that people could place over a photo of themselves with the hashtag #ilovemyballs.

Content can also be created by utilizing a new feature of a social media platform as was the case in "The Voice of Hunger," a campaign for Swiggy, a food delivery service in India, by Dentsu Webchutney. The campaign utilized Instagram's voice note feature to have users send voice memos to earn a chance to win a year's worth of food vouchers. Each day for five days, participants competed in challenges to create an Instagram voice note in the shape of various food items. The campaign also used a hashtag for social (#SwiggyVoiceofHunger) and influencers like Rohan Joshi, Srishti Bansal, and TheFilmyKudi.

A social media feature can also be altered to encourage user-generated content. Glade's "Veiled Snapchat Lens" by Ogilvy Chicago allowed women in Saudi Arabia a way to express themselves through a Snapchat lens that would normally not work if part of a woman's face was covered by a veil. Saudi women shared content widely using the filter, doubling the normal share rate for the region.

Some campaigns inspired the creation of a product and set it within a community of other fans. National Geographic's campaign "Planet or Plastic?" built a community by tapping partner Wattpad, a platform that offers an established online community of user-generated writers and readers. The campaign inspired users to write and engage with stories related to plastic use, resulting in more than 6,000 stories created.

Other content inspired by campaigns included videos from video game footage and changed profile names on social media platforms. #CodNation, a campaign for the video game Call of Duty by Activision, rebranded the community of gamers to celebrate their creativity and passion. Working with 72andSunny, the game company launched a studio to write and edit hundreds of films based on user footage, which inspired the community of users to follow with 25,000 of their own films.

The public service announcement #DefytheName by BBDO New York showed personalities being introduced or introducing themselves with the taunts they received while growing up, such as "skinny piece of crap" (Tony Hawk) and "weirdo" (Sarah Silverman), with the message to not let bullying define a person. The goal of the campaign was to have people change their names on sites like Twitter to include the names that were used to bully them. For example, Monica Lewinsky, who was behind the campaign, embraced her online name of "Monica Chunky Slut Stalker That Woman Lewinsky."

Campaign influencers

Campaigns recognized in the PR Lions and Social & Influencer Lions generally utilized well-known influencers who have transcended their respective realms of sports, film, television, or music to achieve mainstream appeal. These types of influencers are often chosen because entrants have large campaign budgets. These campaigns are also from categories that specifically judge on the use of an influencer who has widespread influence and familiarity.

Some of these campaigns used one influencer to deliver the key message or to participate in a stunt that attracts online commentary. To encourage people to eat prawns with their whiskers intact, Pescanova along with agency LOLA MullenLove created online buzz by having Spanish football coach and former player Vicente del Bosque shave his famous mustache, which created an online buzz about his motivation. After much speculation and media attention, an ad poking fun at a clean-shaven del Bosque not being recognized finally revealed that Pescanova was behind the new look with the message "Choose the Moustache."

Bra brand Berlei with J. Walter Thompson used Serena Williams singing the Divinyls' song "I Touch Myself" to encourage women to perform breast self-exams. "NBA Sellouts" by Deutsch for Hulu featured basketball star Joel Embiid in a humorous campaign where he purportedly changed his nickname from "The Process" to "Hulu Has Live Sports" and is shown signing basketballs with his new nickname.

Weber Shandwick's campaign "Deep Fraud" for HSBC UK included Rachel Riley, a British television personality known for her math abilities. The campaign launched a video where Riley "admitted" to lacking math skills and having had answers fed to her via an earpiece. After one day, it was revealed that the video was a "deep fake" and that her mouth movements had been digitally altered and voice dubbed. The stunt was used to alert the public about the sophisticated technique of online scam artists.

"The Life Saving Soap Operas" focused on low rates of organ donation in Peru by modifying story lines in two soap operas. In this pop culture crossover, after a lead character in one soap opera was killed, it was discovered that he was an organ donor. Then his organ saved the life of a character in another soap opera. This campaign, by Grey for the Peruvian Ministry of Health, was discussed in media and is attributed to saving 11 lives in the first week after the campaign.

Instead of having the influencer as the centerpiece of the campaign, other campaigns used influencers to further amplify the message. "Sonríe Venezuela" by Venmundo turned the stars in the Venezuelan flag upside down to look like a smile. This optimistic symbol during a time of chaos in the country united migrant Venezuelans around the world. Celebrity influencers, including pop stars Greeicy and Carlos Vives, played a significant role in promoting the message of this campaign.

The campaign "Life Lolli" by BBDO Dusseldorf GmbH involves a heart-shaped lollipop on a cotton swab that can be sucked and then returned to add the potential donor to the bone marrow registry. The accompanying website links to Instagram posts of influencers with thousands to hundreds of thousands of followers licking their Life Lolli lollipop.

"Instrument of Hope" by Publicis New York created a trumpet from bullet casings to continue the conversation about gun violence. The campaign was conducted on behalf of ShineMSD, a nonprofit that uses arts to heal the Parkland community after the school shooting at Marjory Stoneman Douglas High School. While on tour, the trumpet has been played by well-known musicians such as Big Bad Voodoo Daddy, Keyon Harrold, and Amos Lee.

"Ha(u)te Couture" by fashion brand Diesel ends with the tagline: "The more hate you wear, the less you care." This campaign, which encourages regular people to confront hurtful online comments by literally wearing them, featured influencers such as Bella Thorne, Gucci Mane, and Yovanna Ventura. This campaign also included Nicki Minaj who headlined a special event at Milan Fashion Week, an appearance cryptically announced on her Instagram.

Other campaigns sought organic relationships with influencers. "Refurbished Tweets" by Back Market, a French seller of refurbished phones, created a humorous campaign with agency BETC Paris to target the U.S. market. They found old tweets where celebrity influencers talked about their excitement for new phones, which are now outdated. For example, the company responded to a 2012 tweet from Kylie Jenner expressing anticipation for her new iPhone 5 by sending her a refurbished phone and replying to the tweet that the phone was on its way. The campaign targeted 311 celebrity tweets and sent out 187 refurbished smartphones.

Some campaigns used a combination of well-known celebrity influencers and regular people. The campaign for "Luna Bar Equal Pay Campaign" by Golin featured television journalist Catt Sadler interviewing four executive women from different sectors about salary negotiation in order to achieve equal pay. The accompanying website offered more resources for women.

"LifeStreams" for the Peruvian Cancer Foundation by Wunderman Thompson Lima recruited influencers to allow a one-day takeover of their Instagram account through the use of the double streaming feature called "Go Live with a Friend." The top half of an influencer's face was paired with the bottom half of the face of a child with cancer. Followers of the influencer then heard the voice of the child asking for support.

Finally, some campaigns make influencers of ordinary people. Visit-Finland, which promotes the "happiest country in the world," developed the campaign "Rent a Finn," which involved recruiting regular Finns as the first official happiness guides for the country. The campaign also encouraged visitors to use the #rentafinn hashtag to locate other Finns willing to serve as guides.

"Stop Mithani" for HDFC Bank by Leo Burnett India introduced viewers to Jyotindra Mithani, who has donated blood a record number of times in the last 30 years. At age 65, doctors suggested that donating blood could be fatal for him, but Mithani expressed no intention to stop. The campaign challenged 100,000 donors to step up in an effort to stop Mithani from donating.

A popular trend in the fashion industry is collaborations between two well-known brands, but "Diesel x Mustafa" by Publicis Italy was a collaboration between Diesel and an unlikely and ironic partner, a popular kebab shop in Berlin owned by a man named Mustafa. Diesel clothing was designed and sold online that featured the kebab shop logo.

Conclusion

The Cannes Lions campaigns, although not representative of all creative work around the globe, provide some insights on how brands build community, engage consumers to create content, and use influencers. Communities are often inspired to form around a social media hashtag or in response to a stunt. Sometimes brand communities are built or conversations occur in a space where a community already exists or around a public concern. The content created can be organic content such as tweets or Instagram posts or co-created through provided graphics. Some content allows users to try a new social media feature or an existing feature in a new way. The user-generated content can also emerge from a community that already exists. Finally, many of the recognized campaigns use well-known celebrities as influencers, who can either deliver the key campaign messages or help amplify them. Some campaigns try to build organic relationships with well-known influencers, others use a combination of established and unknown influencers, and finally, some locate ordinary people to inspire others.

References

Cannes Lions. (2019). *Cannes Lions announces 2019 award entry numbers*. Retrieved from www.canneslions.com/about/news/cannes-lions-announces-2019-award-entry-numbers

Resources

Many of the Cannes Lions entry videos and shortlisted campaigns reviewed for this chapter are available on the following websites:

Adforum's PR Lions Videos. Retrieved from www.adforum.com/award-organi zation/6650183/showcase/2019/winners?tab_category=PR

Adforum's Social & Influencer Lions Videos. Retrieved from www.adforum.com/ award-organization/6650183/showcase/2019/winners?tab_category=Social+%26+ Influencer

PR Lions Shortlist. Retrieved from www.bizcommunity.com/f/1906/PR_Lions_-_ Cannes_Lions_2019_Shortlist.pdf

Social & Influencer Lions Shortlist. Retrieved from www.bizcommunity.com/f/ 1906/Social_&_Influencer_Lions_-_Cannes_Lions_2019.pdf

The Stable's Social & Influencer Lions Videos. Retrieved from www.thestable.com. au/cannes-lions-shortlist-2019-social-influencer/

4 Influencer strategies and political PR

An AOC case analysis

Ashley Hinck and Leslie Rasmussen

In June 2018, Alexandria Ocasio-Cortez (AOC) beat incumbent Joseph Crowley during the Democratic primary race for the House of Representatives seat for New York's 14th district, covering Queens and the Bronx (Goldmacher & Martin, 2018). The win was a shocking upset. Crowley was well established: He had served ten terms and was widely considered one of the top Democrats in the House. Ocasio-Cortez, on the other hand, was largely unknown. But Ocasio-Cortez's significance and fame didn't fade after her well-publicized upset. Well into her first year in office, Ocasio-Cortez maintained support from her district while also cultivating a national following – a remarkable feat considering she is a freshman representative.

The strategies Ocasio-Cortez used to achieve this differ significantly from traditional public relations strategies used by politicians like Crowley. Research in political science, public relations, and Internet studies typically assumes social media is best used to mobilize and activate publics – that is, politicians and political groups use Internet tools to achieve logistical goals, like organizing events, donating money, and disseminating information. We contend that Ocasio-Cortez took a different approach. Rather than relying on social media to achieve the instrumental needs of her publics, she used social media to build relationships. In other words, rather than using social media as a politician, Ocasio-Cortez used social media as an influencer.

In this chapter, we focus on Ocasio-Cortez's Instagram account, @ocasio2018, which has just under 4 million followers. This account began as her personal account, with posts going back to 2012, but was rebranded for her transition to influencer-politician. Ocasio-Cortez also has an official Instagram account as a representative under @repocasiocortez, but that account is seldom used. Her most significant account as an influencer and politician is her @ocasio2018 account. For this chapter, we examined Ocasio-Cortez's Instagram activity from when she announced her candidacy in June 2017 to July 2019. We examine Ocasio-Cortez's Instagram engagement by first examining the literature on social media used in

DOI: 10.4324/9780429327094-5

politics, before outlining three influencer strategies Ocasio-Cortez uses to build relationships with her followers and constituents. Lastly, we identify takeaways for practitioners and scholars.

Literature review: politicians' and influencers' use of social media

Early scholars and public commentators had hoped that the Internet would democratize politics (Benkler, 2006; see, e.g., Papacharissi, 2002). They had hoped that the Internet would allow any citizen to speak – a stark contrast to a mass media model that required significant resources and access in order to be heard. But scholars in political science, political communication, and Internet studies have largely found that hope unrealized. Examining the structure of political websites in the 2000s, Matthew Hindman (2009) found that, despite the ability for anyone to speak, only elites were actually heard, a situation that mirrored the mass media public sphere. Jennifer Stromer-Galley (2014) finds that the same extends to presidential campaigns. Scholars have instead located the transformative potential of the Internet in its ability to streamline logistical processes (Hindman, 2009; Karpf, 2012). The Internet made organizing volunteers and taking donations easier than ever before (see, e.g., Muralidharan, Rasmussen, Patterson, & Shin, 2011). This was the primary lesson of the Howard Dean 2004 campaign, one which Obama later applied as well (Hindman, 2005; Stromer-Galley, 2014). Ultimately, like Hindman (2009), Stromer-Galley argues that political campaigns aim to win elections, not democratize politics. Doing so may mean increased opportunities for interactivity, like polls, videos, and other tools. But, she argues, "there is little strategic advantage for campaigns to enable rich dialogue with citizens about campaign strategy or about policy positions of candidates" (Stromer-Galley, 2014, p. 2). In other words, the Internet may enable citizens to easily donate money or access campaign materials. But campaigns have not used the Internet to democratize the voices of citizens or access to/interaction with political candidates. In this chapter, we argue that the case of Ocasio-Cortez may be challenging that view. Rather than adopting strategies from past campaigns and politicians, Ocasio-Cortez is adopting strategies from online *influencers* and transforming the norms of political engagement as a result.

In 2008, Senft defined influencers as a type of celebrity that has cultivated a large amount of followers on social media.[1] The followers become capital and are eventually used as such for financial gain. Essentially, the followers are a commodity for influencers to build a business. A decade later, Forbes (Wissman, 2018) explained the number of followers is not the primary factor in influencing – it is the engagement between influencer and followers that matters most. Micro-influencers have also emerged, also challenging the previously held norm that number of followers was most important in determining influence. Micro-influencers are those social media influencers with smaller followings ranging from 10,000 to 500,000. Their power lies in the niche audiences who are deeply engaged (Wissman, 2018).

Influencer communication strategies primarily function to build relationships with their followers. Influencers grant their followers access to much of their lives, sharing information about their relationships, their everyday habits, and their beliefs and values (Rojek, 2001). In providing this access, followers come to feel like they know the influencer as a close friend, (Baym, 2012), creating what researchers have termed a parasocial relationship (Dibble, Hartmann, & Rosaen, 2016; Horton & Wohl, 1956). This feeling of closeness is part of what makes influencers so powerful; their followers care deeply about the influencer through a kind of fannish affect (Busse & Gray, 2011; Grossberg, 1992; Van Zoonen, 2005). That means that influencer followers aren't just eyeballs on advertisements, rather followers believe, trust, and value the influencer and what the influencer has to say, whether that's a recommendation for a product (Rasmussen, 2018) or a call to donate money to charity (Hunting & Hinck, 2017).

Strategies

We argue that Ocasio-Cortez adopts typical influencer strategies, using them to build a close relationship with her follower-constituents. By doing so, she doesn't use social media in logistical or back-end ways, as most politicians, but rather, uses social media to build relationships with voters. Ocasio-Cortez's Instagram feed 1) shows "unofficial life behind the scenes," 2) shares fan art, and 3) talks to and with her followers-constituents online. Ocasio-Cortez uses these strategies to build relationships while adapting them to a political context, providing authenticity, community, access, and accountability.

First, Ocasio-Cortez shows her "unofficial life behind the scenes" through Instagram posts and stories, providing both authenticity and transparency. For example, on the day of her swearing in to Congress, Ocasio-Cortez posted a picture of two women fixing her hair. This is far from the finished and polished portrait you would typically see in a newspaper or magazine. Rather, it shows the behind-the-scenes life of Ocasio-Cortez. Further, Ocasio-Cortez often films Instagram stories from a car, talking to her follower-constituents about where she is going and what is going on in that moment. The setting of the car adds to a feeling of authenticity – that this view of Ocasio-Cortez behind the scenes is organic, natural, and authentic, rather than planned, posed, and edited. Such authenticity lends a feeling of "realness" and honesty to the relationship she builds with her followers, a key goal for any influencer-celebrity (Duffy, 2017; Ellcessor, 2016). Ocasio-Cortez extends this uniquely to the political context as well. During her first days in office, she created a series of Instagram stories showing her follower-constituents what the two-week orientation was like for a freshman representative. In doing so, she not only showed her own life behind the scenes, as influencers do, but also unveiled important aspects of the political process, previously invisible to constituents. Ocasio-Cortez took users' desires for authenticity from influencers (Duffy, 2017) and transparency from politicians (Bennett, 2008) and met them both in new ways through her Instagram strategies.

Second, Ocasio-Cortez shares fan art created by her follower-constituents, enacting two-way communication and building community. Such art usually depicts Ocasio-Cortez along with a slogan or a quotation, like "Ultimately, feminism is about women choosing the destiny that they want for themselves." Sharing fan-created works is a key component of influencer strategies. Follower-fans of influencers often create this kind of artwork around their favorite influencers/online creators (Davisson, 2016; Gilliland, 2016; Švelch & Krobová, 2016). This is a key aspect of participatory culture – Internet users create and share art and other forms of communication among communities of like-minded people (Benkler, 2006; Jenkins, 2006; Jenkins, Itō, & boyd, 2015). Art like this becomes one way to perform a love of a particular influencer/creator and helps build a sense of community among follower-fans (Turk, 2014). While mass media (and the PR strategies used to target mass media) functions in a one-way direction from politician to constituents, social media gives politician-influencers a chance to enact two-way communication (Benkler, 2006). Ocasio-Cortez engages in two-way communication with her follower-constituents, helping to build a sense of community online.

Third, Ocasio-Cortez frequently talks to and with her follower-constituents on Instagram, providing valuable access. For example, Ocasio-Cortez talks to her constituents on Instagram Live while she cooks instant pot meals like chili and macaroni cheese. During these sessions, Ocasio-Cortez talks about her policy proposals and current political issues and answers follow-up questions via chat. Additionally, she sometimes does this via typed text on Instagram stories. For example, while riding the train from Washington, D.C. to New York, she answered questions about the Green New Deal, favorite podcasts to listen to, and dealing with disagreement and criticism over her policy proposals. While politicians may sometimes host town-hall meetings or community events, these happen most frequently during campaign season. Ocasio-Cortez uses influencer strategies to accomplish the same goal – providing access to the politician – year-round, not only during campaign season. Further, by providing access, Ocasio-Cortez builds intimacy: Ocasio-Cortez enacts an intimate everyday behavior (cooking), a common way for influencers to create feelings of intimacy among their communities (Ellcessor, 2012). By providing access, Ocasio-Cortez also provides education and accountability – she educates her audience about policies and public issues while at the same time positioning herself as accountable to them, their questions, and their concerns. Ocasio-Cortez is not only accessible and accountable through constituent letters/emails or investigative journalism, but her Instagram Live sessions and chats regularly make her accessible and accountable directly to her constituents.

Takeaways for practitioners

Examining Ocasio-Cortez's social media approach provides several takeaways for practitioners. First, practitioners cannot disregard the importance of community building and sharing. Ocasio-Cortez does this in a number of ways, but one strong method is by sharing fan art. Sharing content created by fans shows an appreciation for audiences and serves as a conduit to strengthen parasocial relationships. Accessibility and transparency also work to strengthen the relationship between fan and speaker. Ocasio-Cortez provides a level of perceived accessibility to fans and constituents by providing a behind-the-scenes look at what goes on in government and often in an on-the-fly style. Allowing fans and constituents to ask questions on Instagram and responding to many builds credibility with regard to transparency. Additionally, the two-way communication aids in forming and strengthening relationships. Fans become connected to and more invested in figures when they are accessible and responsive.

While Ocasio-Cortez embraces influencer strategies, she also challenges one: creating the perfect aesthetic. Instead of crafting aesthetically pleasing, near-perfect content, AOC meets her audiences where they are, and in a more organic way. For example, she does not follow a particular scheme; rather, she is close to her phone and speaks directly to people as though she is right there with them. This also intensifies the appearance of accessibility and transparency, and further aids in developing a strong relationship between fans and figures. Rejecting this common practice creates a sense of realness and authenticity.

Takeaways for scholars

The case of AOC offers two lessons for scholars. First, Ocasio-Cortez's social media strategy presents scholars with the challenge of archiving communication in an age of social media posts that are temporary. Instagram stories disappear after 24 hours. Snapchat stories can only be viewed once. Livestreams on Twitch are live and in the moment. For scholars studying social media, public relations, and communication, this presents a challenge. Ocasio-Cortez's case is a reminder that we must archive this communication ourselves, often before we know whether or not a case or research project is actually viable. Second, the case of Ocasio-Cortez's Instagram influencer strategies is a reminder that communication scholars must read widely, across subdisciplines. Without research on PSR, celebrity, fandom, and influencers, it is difficult to understand Ocasio-Cortez's political strategies. This case reminds us, that as communication scholars, we must take both the Internet and fandom seriously.

Conclusion

While we have seen more politicians use social media to communicate with constituents and to mobilize and activate publics, Ocasio-Cortez embraces influencer strategies more enthusiastically than any others. Politicians may dabble in influencer strategies, but Ocasio-Cortez's use is consistent – it is cemented as her brand. Influencers create feelings of intimacy with audiences often by showcasing everyday life, something Ocasio-Cortez regularly embraces. And yet, by disregarding the influencer trend to create a near-perfect aesthetic on social media, Ocasio-Cortez is actually improving her chance to build and connect with her audience. Doing so allows her to appear more authentic, transparent, and accessible, significant accomplishments for any politician.

Note

1 Throughout this chapter, we draw on research that uses the term "influencer" as well as "celebrity." We find that the terms influencer and follower are typically used when examining public relations or marketing (i.e., the brand deals influencers make) and the terms celebrity and fan are used when talking about celebrity communication and branding.

References

Baym, N. (2012). Fans or friends?: Seeing social media audiences as musicians do. *Participations: Journal of Audience & Reception Studies*, 9(2), 286–316.

Benkler, Y. (2006). *The wealth of networks: How social production transforms markets and freedom.* New Haven: Yale University Press.

Bennett, L. (Ed.). (2008). *Civic life online: Learning how digital media can engage youth.* Cambridge, MA: MIT Press.

Busse, K., & Gray, J. (2011). Fan cultures and fan communities. In V. Nightingale (Ed.), *The handbook of media audiences* (pp. 425–553). Malden: Wiley-Blackwell.

Davisson, A. (2016). Mashing up, remixing, and contesting the popular memory of Hillary Clinton. *Transformative Works and Cultures*, *22*. https://doi.org/10.3983/twc.2016.0965

Dibble, J. L., Hartmann, T., & Rosaen, S. F. (2016). Parasocial interaction and parasocial relationship: Conceptual clarification and a critical assessment of measures. *Human Communication Research*, *42*(1), 21–44. https://doi.org/10.1111/hcre.12063

Duffy, B. E. (2017). *(Not) getting paid to do what you love: Gender, social media, and aspirational work*. New Haven and London: Yale University Press.

Ellcessor, E. (2012). Tweeting @feliciaday: Online social media, convergence, and subcultural stardom. *Cinema Journal*, *51*(2), 46–66. https://doi.org/10.1353/cj.2012.0010

Ellcessor, E. (2016). One tweet to make so much noise: Connected celebrity activism in the case of Marlee Matlin. *New Media & Society*, online first, 1–17.

Gilliland, E. (2016). Racebending fandoms and digital futurism. *Transformative Works and Cultures*, *22*. https://doi.org/10.3983/twc.2016.0702

Goldmacher, S., & Martin, J. (2018, June 26). Alexandria Ocasio-Cortez defeats Joseph Crowley in major democratic house upset. *The New York Times*. Retrieved from www.nytimes.com/2018/06/26/nyregion/joseph-crowley-ocasio-cortez-democratic-primary.html

Grossberg, L. (1992). Is there a fan in the house?: The affective sensibility of fandom. In L. A. Lewis (Ed.), *The adoring audience: Fan culture and popular media* (pp. 50–65). New York: Routledge.

Hindman, M. (2005). The real lessons of Howard Dean: Reflections on the first digital campaign. *Perspectives on Politics*, *3*(1). https://doi.org/10.1017/S1537592705050115

Hindman, M. (2009). *The myth of digital democracy*. Princeton: Princeton University Press.

Horton, D., & Wohl, R. R. (1956). Mass communication and para-social interaction. *Psychiatry*, *29*, 215–229.

Hunting, K., & Hinck, A. (2017). "I'll see you in mystic falls": Intimacy, feelings, and public issues in Ian Somerhalder's celebrity activism. *Critical Studies in Media Communication*, *34*(5), 432–448. https://doi.org/10.1080/15295036.2017.1348613

Jenkins, H. (2006). *Convergence culture: Where old and new media collide*. New York: New York University Press.

Jenkins, H., Itō, M., & boyd, d. (2015). *Participatory culture in a networked era: A conversation on youth, learning, commerce, and politics*. Malden, MA: Polity Press.

Karpf, D. (2012). *The MoveOn effect: The unexpected transformation of American political advocacy*. New York: Oxford University Press.

Muralidharan, S., Rasmussen, L., Patterson, D., & Shin, J.-H. (2011). Hope for Haiti: An analysis of Facebook and Twitter usage during the earthquake relief efforts. *Public Relations Review*, *37*(2), 175–177. https://doi.org/10.1016/j.pubrev.2011.01.010

Papacharissi, Z. (2002). The virtual sphere: The internet as a public sphere. *New Media & Society*, *4*(1), 9–27.

Rasmussen, L. (2018). Parasocial interaction in the digital age: An examination of relationship building and the effectiveness of YouTube celebrities. *The Journal of Social Media in Society*, *7*(1), 280–294.

Rojek, C. (2001). *Celebrity*. London: Reaktion Books.

Senft, T. M. (2008). *Camgirls*. Digital Formations. Vol. 4. New York: Peter Lang.

Stromer-Galley, J. (2014). *Presidential campaigning in the internet age*. New York, NY: Oxford University Press.

Švelch, J., & Krobová, T. (2016). Historicizing video game series through fan art. *Transformative Works and Cultures*, *22*. https://doi.org/10.3983/twc.2016.0786

Turk, T. (2014). Fan work: Labor, worth, and participation in fandom's gift economy [symposium]. *Transformative Works and Cultures*, *15*. https://doi.org/10.3983/twc.2014.0518

Van Zoonen, L. (2005). *Entertaining the citizen: When politics and popular culture converge*. Lanham, MD: Rowman & Littlefield.

Wissman, B. (2018, March 2). *Micro-Influencers: The marketing force of the future?* Retrieved from https://www.forbes.com/sites/barrettwissman/2018/03/02/micro-influencers-the-marketing-force-of-the-future/?sh=692c74fe6707

5 Participatory publics

#NASASocial events and fan engagement

Amber L. Hutchins

The National Aeronautics and Space Administration (NASA) is well known for its many innovations and milestones, most notably the Apollo missions of 1961–1972 including the first humans on the moon (Loff, 2015). But the shuttering of the space shuttle program in 2011 and partnerships between NASA and private space companies, most notably SpaceX, the "space race" for a crewed mission to Mars, as well as political and generational shifts, have necessitated new channels and approaches to NASA's public outreach (Sanz, 2017).

Established in 2009, the NASA Social program, the agency's social media brand community, has hosted on-site events aimed at developing relationships with new target publics and increasing visibility for the organization's many research and public initiatives in the post-space shuttle era. NASA Social Attendees serve as ambassadors, sharing their insights via the #NASASocial hashtag across social media platforms with NASA administrators, astronauts, fans, and influencers.

Through a mix of traditional and social media activities, the NASA Social is an example of the usefulness of brand communities for public relations efforts. Although more commonly associated with marketing efforts, brand communities can serve public relations functions and objectives, including media relations activities and creating and maintaining mutually beneficial relationships with highly engaged *participatory publics*.

This chapter will explore the NASA Social program brand community, its interaction with target groups, and engagement of *participatory publics* for media relations functions.

The NASA Social program

As a government agency, NASA is required to communicate information to U.S. citizens. Like many government agencies, social media has become an

DOI: 10.4324/9780429327094-6

important channel for NASA's public affairs activities, including announcements of achievements in research and exploration, garnering public support for its initiative, and furthering the organization's leadership in the global space exploration community (Dunbar, n.d.).

In many ways, NASA's social media is more comparable to Fortune 500 companies than other government agencies. NASA has approximately 500 social media accounts and more than 100 account managers who report to two full-time social media managers. Official NASA social media accounts include flagship accounts, accounts for public facilities including Kennedy Space Center, research field sites, as well as specific programs and projects (Wilson, 2014).

NASA's social media operates as part of the agency's public information directives, to "provide for the widest practicable and appropriate dissemination of information concerning its activities and the results thereof." NASA's social media milestones include the first tweet (Twitter post), Foursquare (geo-location-based social media app) check-in, and astronaut photo "selfie" from space (Yembrick, 2013). NASA's successful and extensive social media efforts have also been recognized by the professional community, including awards and media coverage (Dunbar, 2019).

The NASA Social program is an extension of NASA's social media and public outreach. In 2009, Veronica MacGregor, NASA News and Social Media Manager at the Jet Propulsion Laboratory (JPL), created the first NASA "Tweetup" event, inviting 130 "space enthusiasts" to JPL in California to preview the landing of the "Curiosity" Mars Rover. Attendees shared their experiences with followers via their Twitter accounts and the event was livestreamed for the public. The program was later renamed "NASA Social" and expanded to include events at other facilities in the U.S., including Kennedy Space Center in Florida, Johnson Space Center in Texas, and Wallops Flight Facility in Virginia (MacGregor, 2013). According to NASA:

> NASA Social is a program to provide opportunities for NASA's social media followers to learn and share information about NASA's missions, people, and programs. NASA Social is the next evolution in the agency's social media efforts. Formerly called NASA Tweetup, NASA Social program includes both special in-person events and social media credentials for individuals who share the news in a significant way. This program has brought thousands of people together for unique social media experiences of exploration and discovery.
>
> (Wilson, 2014)

The 1–2-day event includes tours of facilities, launch sites, equipment and vehicles; media briefings and live NASA TV programming; panel presentations and meet-and-greets with NASA employees, administrators and representatives from partnering organizations; and special access to launch viewing sites and other areas, many of which are not open to the general public. NASA Social events are often themed around the organization's major events or initiatives, such as rocket launches or the development of new equipment or vehicles. One of the most notable NASA Social events was the final launch of the space shuttle program (Shuttle Atlantis, Mission STS-135) in 2011, which generated significant media interest as a historic event and included appearances by celebrities and astronauts.

Attendance at NASA Social events is application-only. Although attendees are selected at random, applicants must meet criteria, including U.S. citizenship, and provide links to their social media accounts, follow NASA Social media accounts, and provide a statement of interest. While not all attendees have extensive followings on social media, the criteria to attend creates a baseline of social media and NASA fan activity.

In addition to the event, attendees are invited to join a private Facebook group created and managed by NASA. Attendees can participate in this group before, during, and after the event to communicate with other attendees and share travel logistics, photos, and insights. Outside of the private Facebook group, attendees and the public can use the #NASASocial hashtag, tag the @nasasocial or other NASA Social accounts, or use the hashtag corresponding to the specific event (for example, the 2014 NASA Social event for the TDRS-L satellite launch used the hashtag #TDRSL) in posts across social media platforms.

The NASA Social brand community

Although NASA is fundamentally a U.S. government agency dedicated to scientific research and aerospace endeavors, the organization stands apart from other government agencies in its position as a popular brand. The NASA logo, facilities, and personalities are recognizable among publics on a global scale via the inclusion of NASA vehicles, locations, and its iconic logo in films and television, and NASA-licensed merchandise is available through major retailers as well as their own numerous public facilities and websites.

Other U.S. government agencies have had some success in branding and visibility (whether intentional or not): The Federal Bureau of Investigation (FBI) and the Drug Enforcement Agency (DEA) have high visibility in films and television; the United States Postal Service (USPS) and the United States Mint sell souvenirs and branded products; The Central Intelligence Agency (CIA) has used social media to engage younger and more diverse target publics; The Centers for Disease Control (CDC) and the

Department of Energy and have used popular culture in their external communication.

However, none have "eclipsed" NASA in the combination of these efforts. As such, NASA's public-facing identity is more comparable to private companies than government agencies or nonprofits. Through its well-known achievements and portrayals in film and media, NASA has become synonymous with space exploration, as a symbol and perhaps a brand name for all space exploration, regardless of national sponsorship.

As such, the NASA Social program is effectively a brand community. A brand community can serve the needs of the organization, key publics, consumers, and fans. Loyalty or affinity programs, events, organizational social media accounts, and other tactics have been used to reach and engage those who would become members, informally or formally, of a brand community. Muniz and O'Guinn (2001) defined a brand community as:

> A specialized, non-geographically bound community, based on a structured set of social relationships among admirers of a brand. It is specialized because at its center is a branded good or service. Like other communities, it is marked by a shared consciousness, rituals and traditions, and a sense of moral responsibility.
>
> (2001, p. 412)

The NASA Social program invites the participation of like-minded individuals – NASA *brandfans*, who "exhibit the same devotion to brands and non-media/entertainment organizations like corporate, government, and health-care" (Hutchins & Tindall, 2016, p. 6) – to partake in rituals and traditions in celebration of NASA milestones and significance in history. The NASA Social program also fosters a sense of moral responsibility to the NASA community as a whole – and because of NASA's dual role as a brand and government organization, this can also include global citizenry who benefit directly or indirectly from NASA's research and innovation. With its mix of on-site events and online engagement, the NASA Social program also creates a structure for social relationships across a variety of social media platforms that expand on Muniz and O'Gwinn's description of the use of "computer-mediated environments" for community interactions.

The NASA Social and participatory publics

Brand communities are often associated with marketing efforts, but the NASA Social program is an example of how brand communities can also be used to meet public relations objectives. Scholler and Frohlich (2016) explained the advantages of a brand community in corporate communication, where the organization is not seeking a direct monetary exchange. Two of the advantages that are relevant to the NASA Social program include:

- Brand communities allow companies to interact with various target groups directly and indirectly.
- Brand communities create positive communication about the brand that can also be perceived by mass media.

(p. 73)

Interacting with various target groups

According to NASA, the purpose of the NASA Social program is to engage new and diverse audiences and build a community of advocates, worldwide in person and virtual participation (Yembrick, 2013). As a whole, NASA has sought specifically to connect with younger publics who might not have the generational connection to NASA that previous generations had, especially Baby Boomers who recall the historic Apollo missions as a significant part of their childhood. As one NASA presentation pointed out, Millennials and Gen Z are participatory users of social media who value diversity and storytelling ("Generation Y Perspectives," n.d.).

Attendees have an opportunity to directly interact with NASA administrators and personnel on site, and social media followers have an opportunity to interact with both groups, thus humanizing the relationships and increasing the strength of ties between publics and the organization. Unlike other NASA community engagement programs aimed specifically at educators and science experts, such as the Solar System Ambassador program, NASA Social events attract publics from a variety of generations and occupations. For example, attendees of the 2014 TDRS-L NASA Social included science fiction authors, engineers, photographers, theme park podcasters, as well as undergraduate and graduate students in aerospace and other sciences.

The NASA Social program creates an opportunity for the organization to build relationships with a variety of target groups, including *participatory publics* – publics who are active producers as well as consumers of content, members of online communities, and invested in authentic relationships with organizations beyond commercial brands (including government agencies). As NASA Social Attendees are selected from applicants who are active in social media, this can help extend the agency's reach to new or underserved target groups.

Creating positive communication that can be perceived by mass media

Attendees serve multiple roles at NASA Social events, including performing media relations activities traditionally executed by reporters, public relations, or public affairs specialists. Alongside credentialed reporters, attendees are provided with media kits and press materials, and are sometimes invited to attend press conferences for a media "scoop." According to MacGregor, "The kind of access we give fans for these events are at the level of what we'd give a U.S. senator" (Epstein, 2015). As one attendee of the 2014 TDRS-L satellite launch described in a blog post about the event:

> Next on the agenda was something described only as "Special News Conference." We walked to another building in the press center, this one a lot larger and better appointed, and took seats in the audience of NASA's TV studio along with a bunch of real [sic] other journalists. The event turned out to be the official announcement by Sierra Nevada Corporation that they have signed contracts to conduct Dream Chaser operations in Florida, beginning with an orbital test launch. This is very big news for Dream Chaser, Sierra Nevada, Kennedy Space Center, and the state of Florida and we were privileged to be there for the announcement.
>
> (Levine, 2014)

Media relations remain a core function of public relations efforts, but as media models evolve and publics become increasingly more engaged, traditional techniques must be reevaluated. The Public Relations Society of America outlines several Knowledge, Skills, and Abilities (KSAs) guidelines for best practices for public relations practitioners in media relations, news sensibility, understanding media, and use of distribution methods (PRSA, 2015). The NASA Social demonstrates how KSAs can be expanded to consider *participatory publics* as media content creators, who are self-publishing media outlets themselves, sometimes with greater reach than traditional outlets (understanding media), and nano-influencers with the potential to reach strategic and emerging target publics. By providing exclusive access and breaking news (news sensibility), NASA Social events create opportunities for attendees to share first-person storytelling via their own social media channels (distribution methods) to the NASA brand community and beyond, effectively amplifying and humanizing the organization's key messages and narratives.

Conclusion

As publics increasingly become more involved in online communities, and relationships with *participatory publics* become more important to organizations, it is worthwhile to consider the conceptual and functional role of public relations in the creation, development, and management of effective brand communities. As an extension of NASA's successful and extensive social media programs, the NASA Social combines online and offline efforts to extend the agency's narratives to new publics and creates opportunities for a more robust and active relationships. Through exclusive access and experiences, the NASA Social program's brand community supports public relations efforts, including direct and indirect communication with publics and positive communication with *participatory publics* that can be communicated to the media. In addition, the NASA Social program demonstrates expansion of PRSA's KSAs in media relations, understanding of media, and distribution methods in the evolving media climate, through engagement of *participatory publics*.

References

Dunbar, B. (2019). *NASA social media efforts win Two Webby Awards*. Retrieved from www.nasa.gov/press-release/nasa-social-media-efforts-win-two-webby-awards

Dunbar, B. (n.d.). *The birth of NASA*. Retrieved from www.nasa.gov/exploration/whyweexplore/Why_We_29.html

Epstein, A. (2015). *How a bunch of space geeks at NASA won the internet*. Retrieved from https://qz.com/420267/how-a-bunch-of-government-space-geeks-at-nasa-won-the-internet/

Generation Y Perspectives. (n.d.). Retrieved from www.nasa.gov/pdf/214672main_KPainting-GenY_rev11.pdf

Hutchins, A. L., & Tindall, N. T. (2016). New media, new media relations: Building relationships with bloggers, citizen journalists, and engaged publics. In *Public relations and participatory culture: Fandom, social media and community engagement*. London and New York: Routledge Taylor and Francis Group.

Levine, D. (2014). *Best field trip ever!* Retrieved from www.daviddlevine.com/2014/01/best-field-trip-ever-long-tdrs-l-nasasocial/

Loff, S. (2015). *The apollo missions*. Retrieved from www.nasa.gov/mission_pages/apollo/missions/index.html

MacGregor, V. (2013). *NASA celebrates anniversary of first tweetup*. Retrieved from www.jpl.nasa.gov/news/news.php?feature=3662

Muniz, A., & O'Guinn, T. (2001). Brand community. *Journal of Consumer Research*, *27*(4), 412–432. Oxford University Press.

PRSA. (2015). *Accreditation readiness review guide and materials*. Retrieved from www.prsaaccredidation.org/resources/documents/apr-rr-candidatw-instructions.pdf

Sanz, A. (2017). *Private companies drive "new space race" at NASA center.* Retrieved from www.apnews.com/3bd8bf7a3d834a3ebebfed266d13aab8

Scholler, C., & Frohlich, R. (2016). Brand communities in social media: Strategic approaches in corporate communication. In A. L. Hutchins & N. T. Tindall (Eds.), *Public relations and participatory culture: Fandom, social media and community engagement.* London and New York: Routledge Taylor and Francis Group.

Wilson, J. (2014). *Social media at NASA.* Retrieved from www.nasa.gov/socialmedia

Yembrick, J. (2013). *NASA social media, 2012 edition.* Retrieved from www2.slide share.net/nasa/social-media-at-nasa-2012-edition

6 How hashtag activism and community upended R. Kelly's traditional litigation public relations push

Natalie T. J. Tindall

Overview of R. Kelly's career

The years of 2018, 2019, and 2020 are the extramundane years of reckoning for Robert Kelly, the R&B musician known as R. Kelly. Famous in the 1990s and early 2000s for a cornucopia of lascivious love songs ("You Remind Me Of My Jeep" and "Bump N Grind"), gospel ditties ("I Believe I Can Fly"), and hip-hop bops ("Fiesta"), Kelly has been under multiple clouds of dark scandals for years. What made 2018 and 2019 different was the press of the #MuteRKelly movement and the launch of the *Surviving R. Kelly* documentary, and the federal and state charges that have landed R. Kelly without gigs and behind bars.

Legal issues facing R. Kelly

This is not a new circumstance for R. Kelly or his legal team. In the 1990s and 2000s, he has bounced in and out of court. For 19 years, Jim DeRogatis has documented the abuses and allegations against R. Kelly. In 2019, dream hampton produced and directed *Surviving R. Kelly*, a six-part documentary that outlined fresh and old allegations about R. Kelly. Almost 27 million people watched the documentary, and the hashtag topped Twitter for many days. Within days, Kim Foxx, the Cook County State's Attorney, held a press conference asking additional victims to come forward, and his record label RCA dropped him. He has been charged with 10 counts. More evidence of his crime in multiple jurisdiction have popped up. One year later, a follow-up to that documentary featuring new survivors aired on Lifetime.

Relevant literature

Hashtag activism

Hashtags were created in 2007 when a Twitter user proposed the merged use of the pound symbol and key words (https://blog.hootsuite.com/how-

DOI: 10.4324/9780429327094-7

to-use-hashtags/). Since then hashtags have become an efficient and effective shortcut to find a community, watch television programs, and discover new ideas. Hashtags have also emerged as a site for community building and social action. In their 2020 book on hashtag activism, authors Jackson Bailey and Foucault Welles believe that activism and online social movements created through these digital shorthands work "to naturalize and center the politics of counter publics, develop repertoires of political connection, and attract allies" (p. 185).

Hashtag activism fits into the capacities typology. Tufekci (2017) proposed narrative capacity, disruptive capacity, and electoral and/or institutional capacity. The narrative capacity is the movement's ability to craft its own narrative, "to frame its story on its own terms, to spread its worldview" (p. 192). Disruptive capacity is engaged when the social movements ministrations interrupt the status quo of the organization or brand (p. 197): "This interruption may take form of a momentary intervention . . . or a prolonged disruption . . . Sometimes disruption of business is done through boycotts or refusal to cooperate." The final component is institutional capacity or the ability of the movement to have changes enacted through internal and external means.

A high-profile example of hashtag activism in action against a celebrity is the launch and use of #FastTailedGirls, the first hashtag to surface successfully about R. Kelly.[1] This particular hashtag uses "culturally resonant language and phrases" (Clark, 2015, p. 206) that allow this conversation to happen within the personal communities and "cultural conversation" (Clark, 2015) of Black Twitter. In 2013, two Black female Twitter users coined that hashtag when R. Kelly and Lady Gaga performed at the American Music Awards; this performance prompted a vigorous Twitter debate about "his continued celebrity despite his predatory sexual behavior toward Black girls" (Jackson, Bailey, & Welles, 2020, p. 41). The 2013 hashtag and tweets worked to "focus on the sexualization of Black girls within the Black community . . . and make clear connections to and critiques of larger white supremacist tropes that have constructed Black women and girls as 'always rapeable'" (p. 38).

A component of hashtag activism is boycotting, and, in the Web 3.0 age, an active boycott now (wrongfully or rightfully, depending on the scholar) equates to the calling for the "cancellation" of problematic favorites – celebrities, influencers, brands, and the like – to draw attention to current and prior bad acts. Bromwich (2018) defined cancel culture as "an act of withdrawing from someone whose expression – whether political, artistic, or otherwise – was once welcome or at least tolerated, but no longer is" (para. 8).

Cancellation is not the same as the widely used term, "cancel culture." Cancel culture is the idea that a person or brand can be "culturally blocked from having a prominent public platform or career" (Romano, 2019, para. 1). According to Romano (2019), who wrote a social history of cancel culture:

"While the terminology of cancel culture may be new and most applicable to social media through Black Twitter, in particular, the concept of being canceled is not new to black culture," Anne Charity Hudley, the chair of linguistics of African America for the University of California Santa Barbara, told Vox. Hudley, who studies black vernacular and the use of language in cultural conversations like this one, described canceling as "a survival skill as old as the Southern black use of the boycott."

What's more, it promotes the idea that Black people should be empowered to reject the parts of pop culture that spread harmful ideas. "If you don't have the ability to stop something through political means, what you can do is refuse to participate," she said. Within this case, I prefer to think of the hashtag activism deployed against R. Kelly in alignment with a "calling out" via a boycott that focuses on his actions and the empowering actions of others that allowed him to operate without regard for others (Velasco, 2020). The goal is not to erase R. Kelly from the public discourse via deplatforming or public shame (Beiner, 2021; Ronson, 2015). Rather, the primary intentions were to bring sunshine onto the darkest parts of his story, to highlight the lack of interest on the part of law enforcement, and to highlight the injustices his victims had to endure. Or, as Clark (2020) stated, this hashtag activism toward R. Kelly is the "application of useful anger" to address and reframe societal issues:

> The absence of deliberation in chastising bad actors, misconstrued as the outcome of cancel culture, is a fault of the elites' inability to adequately conceive of the impact social media connectivity has for shifting the power dynamics of the public sphere in the digital age.
>
> (p. 4)

What is litigation public relations?

Hashtags exist outside of the realm of traditional media, which means that the work of practitioners working with defense clients or clients in crisis expands to deal with both social and digital media as well as pitching and navigating journalists' editorial demands. The digital landscape in which hashtag activism thrives has shifted the work and promise of litigation public relations.

An understudied area of public relations, litigation public relations, emerged in the 1980s (Gower, 2006). Haggerty (2003) in his tactical book on litigation public relations considered the field to be a management function: "managing the communications process during the course of any legal dispute or adjudicatory proceeding so as to affect the outcome or its impact on the client's overall reputation" (p. 2, found in https://doi.org/10.1016/j.pubrev.2017.09.001). Gower, basing her definition on the works of others, framed litigation public relations as "the management of the communications process during the course of any legal dispute or adjudicatory proceeding so as to affect the outcome or its impact on the client's overall reputation" (pp. 100–101).

According to Lerbinger (2019), the intentional goal for litigation public relations and its aims are "to reinforce a case's legal strategy to ensure a win and to reduce damage to an organization's credibility" (p. 261). Xifra (2012) proposed that a continuum of litigation public relations strategies exist, which include pretrial public relations strategies, strategies during the trial, and posttrial public strategies, all of which hinge on media relations practices and planning. Toledano, Peleg, and Drori (2017) found in their interviews with attorneys and public relations practitioners that ground was ceded to the PR team when it came to social media:

> The speed by which rumours and misleading information is spread online results in more cases of "trial by the media." This not only makes a fair trial nearly impossible but means that regardless of the result of the trial the accused might not be able to live the rest of their life without intense public scrutiny. The nature of public comments on social media increases the need of clients for communication services.
>
> (p. 1080)

Given its intentions, litigation public relations rests on a foundation of asymmetrical communication and reputation management. Researchers who have examined litigation public relations have viewed it through the lenses of ethics, media relations, and the traditional Grunig and Hunt (1984) models. The cases examined in the research skew toward celebrities and corporations. Reber, Gower, and Robinson (2006) trumpeted the Internet as "an emerging new tool in litigation public relations," and their study examined the three websites of celebrities involved in litigation. At that time, they found that the traditional standards for litigation public relations transferred. Gower (2006) deviated by examining the case of a CEO charged with conspiracy, false reporting, fraud, and money laundering.

> [The] prosecutors in the criminal case against Richard Scrushy . . . . painted a picture of Scrushy in the media as the mastermind of a scheme to defraud small investors and employees out of their life savings. Scrushy, through his Web site and attorneys, portrayed himself as an innocent victim of conniving subordinates and an overzealous prosecuting attorney. The jury ultimately found that although fraud had indeed occurred at the company, the prosecutors had not established beyond a reasonable doubt that Scrushy knew about the fraud.

LPR strategies in practice

Per Gibson (1998), ten fundamental assumptions guide the practice of litigation public relations:

> 1) LPR is inevitable; 2) LPR is a specialized public relations application; 3) LPR can be offensive or defensive; 4) LPR is regulated; 5) LPR is a Constitutional issue; 6) LPR is a communication phenomenon; 7) LPR is inherently unfair; 8) LPR depends on media relations; 9) LPR is a tri-directional relationship among litigants, the media, and the public; and 10) LPR is intrinsically neutral.

Jin and Kelsay (2008) argued that there are two additional strategies that integrate aspects of journalism, legal, and public relations: Information Supply and Strategic Avoidance. Information supply as a strategy allows the practitioner "to present unbiased facts, suggest alternative solutions to problems, as well as make resources available to the publics" (p. 68). On the other hand, practitioners can deploy the strategic avoidance plan of action, which leans on the legal preference of withholding information. Strategic avoidance according to the authors "includes denying while expressing remorse/compassion for the crisis, defeasibility as claiming that the organization did not have the knowledge/ability/control to avoid committing the offensive act, and saying nothing or as little as possible" (p. 67).

Litigation public relations depends on media relations, but media relations has shifted and adapted to a changing age. Although Supa (2014) contended that media relations remained one of the best ways to build and maintain trust and credibility with key audiences, other scholars disagree about the use and effectiveness of media relations. However, audiences who are involved in a crisis or watching a crisis unfold are augmenting the traditional media diet of news outlets and traditional sources; Jin, Liu, and Austin (2011) and others have found that social media allows publics to seek out and obtain information in real time. Also, the social media space allows for reporters to reverse the standard model for media pitching; Waters, Tindall, and Morton (2010) countered that social media allowed for a new practice of media catching, where reporters were pitching existing story opportunities to public relations practitioners, which may not benefit organizations or brands in a crisis. Finally, journalists are conducting temperature checks online, irrespective of that fact the social media does not represent the larger society. McGregor (2019) in her research on journalistic practices during the 2016 elections found that journalists reported trends and online chatter as a reflection of public opinion.

Discussion

How principles and attributes of hashtag activism worked in the R. Kelly case

In 2017, a new hashtag campaign emerged, #MuteRKelly – that was used in conjunction with #FastTailedGirls to trouble the singer's reputation and challenge the continued presence of R. Kelly in the Black musical sphere. The maintenance and existence of these three capacities provide not only visibility and unity but longevity and strategic mindset. For the hashtag activism activated through #MuteRKelly, the disruptive capacity resulted in the boycotting of R. Kelly. As Jackson, Bailey, and Welles (2020) noted:

> [t]his renewed focus on R. Kelly's actions spread the #MuteRKelly and #SurvivingRKelly campaigns that worked to get Kelly's music off the nation's airwaves, taking hashtag activism out of the digital universe and into the analog. The campaign continues to grow and has prompted Sony to sever ties with the singer, as well as consumer boycotts of concerts, streaming services such as Spotify, club spins, and more.
>
> (p. 189)

Hashtag activism works because of its disruptive capacity to interrupt the modus operandi and the status quo; the creators and distributors of the hashtag worked to make it untenable for "those in power to continue as in the past, and to sustain such disruption over time" (p. 199).

How litigation PR worked in the R. Kelly case

R. Kelly employed spokespersons and publicists throughout each of the legal challenges he has faced, and his legal and communications teams only used the litigation public relations strategy of conversing with the traditional media. Of note is his infamous interview with Gayle King. In March 2019, Kelly sat with Gayle King on *CBS This Morning* in an attempt to clear his name. During the interview, he jumped out of his seat and started screaming, "I've been assassinated," and "I'm fighting for my f – king life." These responses became memes and his interview was widely mocked online.

What his PR team did or could have done to mitigate

One of the core assumptions Gibson (1998) proposed for litigation public relations is that the message must be transmitted via the mass media. In this case, the team should have deployed a messaging strategy via surrogates and avoided trying to work through media gatekeepers. Another assumption is that litigation public relations has tri-directional influence and interactions with the general public, the media, and the litigants' representatives. The idea of a singular, mass media no longer exists, so special consideration for understanding the fragmented state of media as well as the segmenting of publics. For any group pursuing litigation public relations, understanding and analyzing your audience through the PESO model would allow for them to find the best channels to counter boycotting actions and to upend traditional media narratives.

Conclusions and takeaways

Traditionally, litigation public relations is a one-way model with three publics of focus. Most litigation relations public relations scholarship occurred prior to the advent of social media, thus limiting their usefulness. The conception of the general public does not exist and this model neglects the concepts of fandom and superfans, viable entities that affect celebrity culture.

In its conception, the protection of the client's reputation is paramount, and the goal for strategists is to counteract negative publicity, ensure balance in the media coverage, defuse a hostile environment, and make the client's viewpoint well known. But what happens when the negative publicity spins out of control after the insertion of litigation public relations?

Media relations is not what it used to be, and current litigation public relations strategy have yet to accommodate the space between prior practice and modern realities. Conducting media interviews may have earned a few snide commentary pieces in the 1990s; now an interview with outbursts a la the R. Kelly–Gayle King interview or with questionable remarks a la Toure's interview with R. Kelly where he asks for a definition of young can result in memes and GIFs that can be used, teased, and remixed through eternity.

Intentional silence as a strategy, the strategic deployment of no comment, may allow the defendant room to make arguments before a court; it will not hold in the court of public opinion (Fitzpatrick, 2000). As Dimitrov (2019 p. 91–92) wrote, "In litigation PR, for example, the problem of intentional silence carries the strain between strict talk, codified in law, and loose talk, the language of PR. 'No comment' sticks with the strict talk. It is the verbal vow of firm, noncommunicative silence. Off-the-record communication is, on the contrary," intentional silence as a strategy. Yet, using social media can also backfire for a brand. In a Facebook Live post, R. Kelly said that he was handcuffed by his destiny.

In summation, R. Kelly provides a case study to understand how old-school traditional litigation public relations strategies and approaches cannot work in a new-school-mediated world. Messages can escape from the gatekeepers and the controllers; images and videos can take on lives of their own. The rhetorical velocity of a moment – whether scripted and intentional or unintended and spur of the moments – can be remixed sonically, textually, and visually for the harm or the good of the litigant's legal case and societal standing.

Note

1 The idea of "fast" relates to the stereotypes that hyper-sexualize and adultify Black girls (Collins, 2004; Jionde, 2019). As Smith (2019) noted, Black girls can be seen as "womanish" or being "too fast, too hot, and waiting for trouble." Research has shown that Black girls are perceived by adults to be less innocent in schools (Epstein, Blake, & Gonzzlez, 2017) and in the criminal justice system (Thompson, 2020).

References

Beiner, A. (2021, April 26). Sleeping woke: Cancel culture and simulated religion. Retrieved from https://medium.com/rebel-wisdom/sleeping-woke-cancel-culture-and-simulated-religion-5f96af2cc107

Bromwich, J. (2018, June 28). Everyone is canceled. Retrieved from https://www.nytimes.com/2018/06/28/style/is-it-canceled.html

Clark, M. D. (2015). Black Twitter: Building connection through cultural conversation. In *Hashtag publics: The power and politics of discursive networks* (pp. 205–218). New York: Peter Lang.

Clark, M. D. (2020). DRAG THEM: A brief etymology of so-called "cancel culture." *Communication and the Public.* https://doi.org/10.1177/2057047320961562.

Collins, P. H. (2004). *Black sexual politics: African Americans, gender, and the new racism*. London: Routledge.

Dimitrov, R. (2019). Communicating off the record. *Public Relations Inquiry*, 1–22. doi:10.1177/2046147X19841565

Epstein, R., Blake, J., & Gonzzlez, T. (2017). Girlhood interrupted: The erasure of black girlss childhood. *SSRN Electronic Journal.* doi:10.2139/ssrn.3000695

Fitzpatrick, K. (2000). Managing legal crises: Strategic communication in the court of public opinion. *Journal of Communication Management*, 4(4), 385–394. https://doi.org/10.1108/eb023535

Gibson, D. C. (1998). Litigation public relations: Fundamental assumptions. *Public Relations Quarterly*, 43, 19–23.

Gower, K. (2006). Truth and transparency. In K. Fitzpatrick & C. Bronstein (Eds.), *Ethics in public relations: Responsible advocacy* (pp. 89–105). Thousand Oaks, CA: Sage Publications.

Grunig, J. & Hunt, T. (1984). *Managing public relations*. New York: Holt, Rinehart and Winston.

Haggerty, J. F. (2003). *In the court of public opinion: Winning your case with public relations*. Hoboken,, NJ: J. Wiley.

Jackson, S. J., Bailey, M., & Welles, B. F. (2020). *Hashtag activism: Networks of race and gender justice*. Cambridge, MA: MIT Press.

Jin, Y., & Kelsay, C. J. (2008). Typology and dimensionality of litigation public relations strategies: The Hewlett-Packard board pretexting scandal case. *Public Relations Review*, 34, 66–69. https://doi.org/10.1016/j.pubrev.2007.11.009

Jin, Y., Liu, B. F., & Austin, L. L. (2011). Examining the role of social media in effective crisis management. *Communication Research, 41*(1), 74-94. doi:10.1177/0093650211423918

Jionde, E. (2019, January 9). *How young, Black girls were hypersexualized in America: And how that enables predators.* Retrieved January 15, 2021 from www.bustle.com/p/how-young-black-girls-were-hypersexualized-in-america-how-that-enables-predators-15727529

Lerbinger, O. (2019). *Corporate communication: An international and management perspective.* Hoboken, NJ: Wiley-Blackwell.

McGregor, S. C. (2019). Social media as public opinion: How journalists use social media to represent public opinion. *Journalism, 20*(8), 1070–1086. doi:10.1177/1464884919845458

Reber, B. H., Gower, K. K., & Robinson, J. A. (2006). The internet and Litigation public relations. *Journal of Public Relations Research, 18*(1), 23–44. doi:10.1207/s1532754xjprr1801_2

Romano, A. (2019, December 30). Why we can't stop fighting about cancel culture. Retrieved from https://www.vox.com/culture/2019/12/30/20879720/what-is-cancel-culture-explained-history-debate

Ronson, J. (2015). *So You've Been Publicly Shamed.* London: Pan Macmillan.

Smith, D., Caruthers, L. E., Fowler, S., & James, J. (2019). Womanish Black girls: *Women resisting the contradictions of silence and voice.* Gorham, ME: Myers Education Press.

Supa, D. W. (2014). A qualitative examination of the impact of social media on media relations practice. *Public Relations Journal, 8.* Retrieved from https://prjournal.instituteforpr.org/wp-content/uploads/2014Supa.pdf

Toledano, M., Peleg, A., & Drori, Z. (2017). Conflict and cooperation between advocates: Lawyers, pr practitioners, and the client's best interest. *Public Relations Review, 43*(5), 1073–1083. doi:10.1016/j.pubrev.2017.09.001

Tufekci, Z. (2017). *Twitter and tear gas: The power and fragility of networked protest.* London: Yale University Press.

Velasco, J. C. (2020). You are cancelled: Virtual collective consciousness and the emergence of cancel culture as ideological purging. *Rupkatha Journal on Interdisciplinary Studies in Humanities, 12,* 1–7. https://dx.doi.org/10.21659/rupkatha.v12n5.rioc1s21n2 and https://doi.org/10.1080/14680777.2018.1456160

Waters, R. D., Tindall, N. T., & Morton, T. S. (2010). Media catching and the journalist–public relations practitioner relationship: How social media are changing the practice of media relations. *Journal of Public Relations Research, 22*(3), 241–264. doi:10.1080/10627261003799202

Xifra, J. (2012). Sex, lies, and post-trial Publicity: The reputation repair strategies of Dominique Strauss-Kahn. *Public Relations Review, 38*(3), 477–483. doi:10.1016/j.pubrev.2012.03.002

7 Multinational Corporate Social Responsibility and diversity

Blizzard Entertainment's *Overwatch*, the *Overwatch* League, and LGBTQ Pride Month

Elaine Venter

Public relations practitioners have been actively debating Corporate Social Responsibility (CSR) over the years (Reeves, 2016; Prezly, 2019). Since becoming popular around the 1970s, the core emphasis of CSR is the expectation that a corporation will adhere to higher standards and goals than purely economic; a corporation will encapsulate ethical behaviors with a specific focus to help society by highlighting and contributing to social values (Reeves, 2016). While CSR promises improved public image, employee satisfaction, and positive impact on societies, there is concern that it easily becomes relegated as a tool only to help build a company's reputation with no earnest intent in helping society beyond increased economic revenue for the corporation, resulting in consumers becoming increasingly skeptical toward public relations messages and CSR initiatives (Reeves, 2016; Hung-Baesecke et al., 2018; White & Fitzpatrick, 2018; Monaghan, 2018). A shortcoming in evaluating the current effects of CSR is that, according to Bortree and Haigh (2018), most CSR studies are conducted in the U.S. on U.S. companies promoting U.S. social values to a predominantly U.S. public. However, the growth of multinational corporations necessitates examining CSR in relation to how relevant and effective they are in addressing cross-cultural challenges. It is through this lens that I examine Blizzard Entertainment and its *Overwatch* League's inclusivity strategy used before, during, and after its Pride Month events to determine if and how it translates LGBTQ rights as a shared social value in its global corporate culture.

Blizzard's *Overwatch* multiplayer video game emphasizes diversity, but what kind of diversity and for which groups specifically? While Blizzard emphasizes a welcoming and safe environment for all, is it possible to do so when the company operates in countries that are antagonistic to LGBTQ rights? Does revealing LGBTQ heroes and hosting an esports LGBTQ Pride

DOI: 10.4324/9780429327094-8

Day do justice to its mission to create a welcoming and safe environment for all, especially the LGBTQ community, or is it just pandering? What are the challenges for a multimillion-dollar global corporation like Blizzard in creating shared values like LGBTQ rights? The examination of these questions is limited to direct and indirect communication from Blizzard Entertainment corporate and affiliated website sources and social media communications from Blizzard Entertainment and affiliated property accounts on Twitter and Instagram.

Blizzard's *Overwatch* and its first LGBTQ hero: Tracer

Blizzard is a multinational corporation, and *Overwatch* is played by over 40 million gamers (Gough, 2019). Gamers are spread across many regional borders, each with their own cultural identities and cultural value systems. However, they are now increasingly connected not only to the game on social media but increasingly on a personal level as well, blurring national boundaries. Blizzard's multiplayer first-person shooter game, *Overwatch*, first attracted this writer with the development team's focus and emphasis on diversity when Blizzard announced the game would feature multiple LGBTQ characters (heroes) at BlizzCon 2015 (Rossi, 2015).

Monaghan (2018) states that if CSR drives corporate mission from the beginning, it becomes easier to implement as a corporate culture and to implement as authentic and genuine support to the public. Blizzard seemed genuine at first when it announced multiple LGBTQ heroes would be in the game in 2015. Players did not have to wait long after launch in May 2016 for the December 16 reveal of Tracer, the first LGBTQ hero, in an online comic. Tracer, a lesbian character, is the hero splashed across marketing since the game's announcement in 2015, becoming the de facto mascot and face of the game. However, never using identifying language in the comic, it had to be clarified that she identifies as a lesbian in a tweet by lead writer Michael Chu.[1] The comic was announced on a Twitter post from the official *Overwatch* video game account @PlayOverwatch, but the post made no direct reference to Tracer's reveal. However, this may have been on purpose to lead up to surprise readers when they read the panel showing Tracer kissing her girlfriend.[2] What is somewhat concerning and detracts from *Overwatch* appearing genuine on the issue of LGBTQ representation is that Chu tweeted out the clarification and not @PlayOverwatch, who also did not retweet Chu. However, an official Blizzard statement was released to journalists:

> As in real life, having variety in our characters and their identities and backgrounds helps create a richer and deeper overall fictional universe

. . . From the beginning, we've wanted the universe of Overwatch to feel welcoming and inclusive, and to reflect the diversity of our players around the world.

(quoted in Serrao, 2016)

Blizzard's *Overwatch* and its second LGBTQ hero: Soldier:76

The next LGBTQ hero was not confirmed until January 2019 in an online short story, *Bestet* (Oh, 2019). In the story, the sniper Ana finds a wounded Soldier:76 and they talk about a man, Vincent. It is alluded that Soldier:76 and Vincent had been in a prior relationship. The release tweet from @ PlayOverwatch was similar in style and tone to the Tracer reveal, leaving the confirmation a surprise in the story.[3] Once again, Soldier was confirmed to identify as a gay man in a clarification tweet from Chu.[4] While Soldier's reveal was generally well accepted, many fans were disappointed in the time span between Tracer and Soldier's reveals and the promise of multiple LGBTQ heroes, fueling fan skepticism of Blizzard's credibility as a company focused on LGBTQ values (Oh, 2019; Valens, 2019).

Local versus global CSR management

The time period between reveals of the two heroes are part of situational analysis and Blizzard must take stock of where its global fan base is culturally, socially, and politically and make choices regarding communication on the expectations of the different groups. Research on CSR communication suggests that multiple strategies from direct corporate communication, a spokesperson, to employees, to affiliated organizations and partners and delivery from official press releases to social media can be used to implement a message to a certain audience most effectively (Kim & Ferguson, 2014; Reeves, 2016; Bortree & Haigh, 2018; Hung-Baesecke et al., 2018). Blizzard strategically allowed employee social media and official press releases to be more direct about LGBTQ representation in the video game, which does make it easier for the varying regions to pick and choose from those messages to present in their own region. LGBTQ representation is openly discussed in the U.S. – Blizzard's global headquarters – than in other parts of the world where Blizzard's *Overwatch* is not only played, but Blizzard operates offices worldwide and has become beholden not only to local cultural customs but law as well.

Blizzard's multicommunication strategy answers two questions: 1) how do different audiences in different regions prefer to receive communication and 2) how does it help balance the cultural, social, and political differences in each region that mitigates and prevents issues with the public or regional governments? Hung-Baesecke et al. (2018) note that American consumers – who tend to identity as an individualist culture in a Western society – prefer accessing CSR information through a variety of communication channels, while Chinese consumers – who tend to identify as a collectivist culture – prefer official channels, but both consumers noted the importance of social media platforms for corporate information. While Blizzard could have announced their LGBTQ heroes in 2015 as a general statement, specific reveals and Pride events have been strategic in balancing different consumer national diversity and government legal compliance, especially in countries like China, South Korea, and Russia where LGBTQ issues face opposition – more so from the governments themselves than players who disagree with LGBTQ, since they are not affected in-game by any clear LGBTQ symbology or voice-lines from the heroes. The Tracer comic was blocked in Russia due to strict anti-LGBTQ laws, which bans "gay propaganda" made viewable to minors (BBC Newsbeat, 2016). China does not have such clear phrasing with a cybersecurity law containing a "social morality" note that leaves the decision to censor something or not up to the corporations (Griffiths, 2019).

Essentially, in the Tracer comic case, Blizzard is following Russian law and when in doubt as to whether they may be subject to any local law, it will probably err on the side of caution, but at what price? In an era before the Internet and social media, it was easier to balance different multinational corporate messages in different regions making it easier to perform lip-service CSR. However, in a global arena where consumers are connected through social media, can a transnational company, especially, balance genuine CSR in one region where that social value is not important or even counter to the social, cultural, or political values of another? Blizzard's attempt to balance all these intricate spheres is best seen by examining communication in their esports arena.

Blizzard's *Overwatch* League and LGBTQ Pride Month

For those unfamiliar with professional esports, there are a wide variety of different professionally competitive leagues. *Overwatch* is one game well suited to competitive play, which is already a feature of the multiplayer team-based structure where each team is composed of six main players and each team gets three rounds to win an objective on a map. In OWL, professional city-based teams across the globe are created and managed similar to other professional sports. Currently, OWL is made up of 20 international teams and a season of play includes up to 280 matches where teams are paired up in brackets against one another on a scheduled day from February culminating in playoffs and then the grand final in the fall.[5] Each team signs a franchise contract with Blizzard, while a team contract is negotiated between teams and players, and then players must sign and abide by a Blizzard Code of Conduct.[6]

LGBTQ Pride Month honors the anniversary of the Stonewall Riots which took place in in New York in June of 1969. Members of the LGBTQ community stood up against police brutality and corruption in a three-day riot spurring a global queer rights movement. While Blizzard's *Overwatch* has special events celebrated in-game featuring skins and voice-lines for events like Summer Games (in honor of the 2016 Rio Summer Olympics), Anniversary (celebrating game's launch), Halloween Terror, Winter Wonderland, and Lunar New Year (now including both Chinese and Korean cultural designs), Pride is not celebrated in-game. Instead, Blizzard honors LGBTQ gamers through their professional esports league with the *Overwatch* League (OWL) Pride Day. And, there is good reason for this: while OWL games are streamed online, OWL esports broadcasting looks like any other sport with casters, desk analysts, interviews with players, and even fans in an arena. However, it also includes splitting broadcasts by region. A master stream sends information to different regions. Different regions may have different shot callers (announcers who describe the action) and desk analysts to localize a broadcast to their region's specific audience of OWL, which includes language and other localization needs – cultural contexts. The master broadcast that originates in the U.S. can be edited as it moves to the other regions. It is more difficult to edit out in-game design per region for a multiplayer game like *Overwatch* than it is to edit a broadcast signal.

The first Pride Day was in the inaugural OWL season in 2018. During this time, Blizzard's OWL posted a news article[7] announcing the event noting that attendees would receive a special Blizzard Pride wristband, which was not for sale. However, in 2019, Blizzard announced the sale of Pride products both through the parent corporation and OWL, which would benefit the Trevor Project, a national nonprofit focused on preventing suicide of LGBTQ youth. Some see this "rainbow merchandise" as capitalist commodification of the movement with corporations benefiting from revenue and taking advantage of good PR and reputation with little risk or give-back to the LGBTQ community (Joseph, 2019). Others accept corporate involvement and products as LGBTQ rights mainstreaming regardless of whether its altruistic or not. Rainbow merchandise can be an excellent way for a nonprofit to fundraise money and help many LGBTQ people, and if a corporation partners with genuine intent and communicates the beneficiaries of the partnership, consumers are less likely to be skeptical and negative toward the cause (Monaghan, 2018).

While fans seemed genuinely happy and interested in the merchandise, there were questions about where the money would go. It was not made clear in the official OWL news article[8] or even in an OWL League Minute tweet[9] advertising Pride Day – which only mentioned the bandana and the Pride shirts for sale – if sales would benefit any LGBTQ organizations. The only official social media posts that featured news and information about the pin were a Blizzard tweet[10] – the only tweet from this account concerning anything Pride – and an Instagram post.[11]

The news release made note of inviting two local LGBTQ organizations to the arena, QWEERTY Gamers[12] and Gay Gaming Professionals, and listed viewing parties hosted by LGBTQ gaming nonprofits and organizations where Blizzard provided swag in four cities, providing links to each of the nonprofits and organizations, which was repeated in 2019 only updating watch party events and organizations. However, while the Blizzard press piece named organizations and provided links to them, no official social media posts mentioned QWEERTY Gamers or Gay Gaming Professionals. QWEERTY Gamers posted two tweets using brand hashtags and tagged OWL, which showed no engagement from any Blizzard accounts. The 2018 Pride broadcast[13] had some mention of LGBTQ topics and images featuring a clip of one watch party in London, but the 2019 broadcast was even more open about Pride featuring an LGBTQ OWL superfan. The broadcast also featured scenes of several watch parties of the organizations mentioned in the news article. However, nothing on the official social media accounts of the game or the esports league were posted about the two LGBTQ organizations and no retweets from their accounts were made to the official accounts leading up to the event.

The official OWL channels beyond the broadcast were relatively limited on coverage. Pride Day saw minimal posts with two Twitter posts linking to a feature article on transgender lesbian and cyberpunk shieldmaiden, Sabriel Mastin, discussing the connection between the game, the league, and her own queer identity:

> [Pride Day] brings visibility to the LGBTQ+ community, uniting queer people and allies in a show of support and love to a community that is often discriminated against at best, and abused or erased at worst . . . That is big to me, knowing you're not alone . . . That's why I'm open on Twitter and panels about being trans. I am here, I am visible, and I am in esports.
>
> (quoted in Savery, 2019)

Visibility has been linked as a key element in helping to make LGBTQ identities more commonly accepted in mainstream society and combatting toxic and homophobic attacks in the esports and larger gaming community. Other posts included a video feature[14] on the Philadelphia Fusion's super fan Alex Parrish who identifies as queer and expressed an intersectional inclusive message for LGBTQ people, women, and people of color, as well as a set of two wrap-up tweets[15] of photos of the day with only two featuring clear, visible Pride symbology. The Instagram account featured even less with only a single post[16] of the photos with the first photo showing Toronto Defiant's Gods with no other posts to indicate Pride Day.

To be fair, OWL does not have many special events outside of traditional sporting events, such as playoffs and grand finals. Another rare special event was the Kit-Kat Rivalry weekend, which saw Los Angeles Valiant host a special event for the end of the regular 2019 season in a special, smaller venue. The event matches did influence standings going into the playoffs but featured several engaging activities with fans and collegiate esports match ups. The official OWL social channel only posted three Kit-Kat Rivalry tweets on the day of the event.[17] In this sense, it can be argued that OWL does a fair job of its posting on special events then since Pride Day seemed no less, really. However, Kit-Kat bars do not face discrimination like LGBTQ gamers. One in three LGBTQ gamers report they faced identity-based harassment in multiplayer games. *Overwatch* seemed to promise representation of and for the LGBTQ community. CSR would indicate that an event, such as Pride Day, would perhaps warrant more attention through official channels. However, keeping limited posts shows no real favoritism and does not necessarily put the parent corporation into trouble with regional issues, legally or socially. However, where the official channels could not seem to post more, the balance comes in OWL city teams and talent took to socials to each show their own support.

Overwatch League teams and talent and LGBTQ Pride Day

There seemed to be more open Pride visibility posts and actions from the OWL teams from both 2018 and 2019. LA Valiant was one of the first esports teams to sign a partnership with a social activist group, You Can Play, a nonprofit dedicated to promoting LGBTQ issues in sports, raising funds for LGBTQ community with the sales of their rainbow team logo patches. Team CEO Noah Whinston made it clear that inclusivity meant sexuality as a core social value for the team:

> For too long, the esports industry has been unfairly characterized as a toxic, unwelcoming environment . . . This assumption runs counter to the core values of the Los Angeles Valiant organization . . . The

message is simple: no matter who you are, who you love, or what gender you identify as – if you can play, you can play.

(quoted in News, 2018)

While many teams changed their logos to rainbow versions on social media in support, LA Valiant was one of the first most visible supporters as well wearing the patches to every game the entire month of June, which they also wore in 2019. For 2019 Pride Day, London Spitfire distributed a special rainbow team logo pin at the event and also posted several tweets featuring pride viewing parties hosted by their official fan association Hangar9 and London Gaymers where the pin was provided as well. However, it is not clear why the pin was not made for sale to raise funds for LGBTQ organizations. LA Gladiators – a second LA-based team – hosted their own fundraiser selling a special team Pride shirt to benefit the Trevor Project, which they featured on their socials as well.[18] While OWL is overall owned and operated by Blizzard, the teams are owned by other corporations and maintain a sense of autonomy. As long as the teams abide by the code of conduct, they have a say in how they may choose to support social values. That gives them more control to be more direct in their own communication on social issues, such as LGBTQ rights. While the Pride support seemed more vocal from OWL teams, there are teams who are in a position where they have to post even more limited on the topic or not at all. For example, several teams are comprised of Korean and Chinese players and because players can move from one team to another, individual players have to be careful about what they post lest it could cost them a position on another team. Four teams are based in China – Shanghai Dragons, Chengdu Hunters, Guangzhou Charge, and Hangzhou Spark – and Seoul Dynasty is based in South Korea. While these teams and players all played in the U.S. studio, their city association comes loaded with the social values of the region.

CSR and the bottom line

Gathering from the evidence presented, it appears that a key issue when a corporation decides to implement CSR initiatives remains their bottom line. In the case of Blizzard, they attempt and appear to be culturally inclusive but remain sensitive about topics that may be perceived as controversial to some fans and other stakeholders where social issues like LGBTQ rights are taboo or too political to touch, which could hurt their bottom line. Reports that the South Korean OWL broadcast edited the event stream to omit references to Pride Day in their broadcast when this year's event featured more visible and open support of Pride and LGBTQ rights does not help the corporation appearing altruistic about LGBTQ community (D'Anastasio,

2019; Bell, 2019). According to an inside source, the edited broadcast was for "cultural reasons" leading to speculation that the reasons refer to South Korea's majority conservative social views on LGBTQ rights (as quoted in D'Anastasio).

While Blizzard's *Overwatch* wants to emphasize LGBTQ diversity, the company seems to be prioritizing profit margin. A coveted growth market for the developer lies in the Asia Pacific market. In 2013 the developer reported 343 million U.S. dollars in revenue; that number tripled in 2018 with over one billion U.S. dollars – *Overwatch* has been a main source of revenue boosts since 2016 (Gough, 2019). However, censorship laws, conservative outrage, and the adage of not being able to please everyone are becoming less accepted reasons to avoid social activism or support, especially for, multimillion-dollar corporations like Blizzard (Campbell, 2017). However, it would simply have been easier for Blizzard to never adopt a diversity strategy for *Overwatch* or OWL at all. Former OWL general manager Susie Kim thought it was inappropriate for the global league to host Pride Day at all because LGBTQ rights are not supported everywhere, especially in Asian countries like China and Korea (Bell, 2019). Kim's statement regarding the seeming cultural insensitivity of Blizzard to host Pride Day was not well accepted, however. So, while Blizzard's OWL certainly allowed countries like South Korea to edit the Pride Day broadcast, the league still hosted a Pride Day.

Conclusion

The line between pandering to consumers and social issues and practicing ethical and truly altruistic CSR can sometimes seem rather blurry. Social issues are no longer isolated within regional boundaries (Castells, 2012). The LGBTQ movement is global and Blizzard *Overwatch* fans are connected to the brand and to one another through social media. Consumers now expect brands to have clear identified social values and to live them if they are to be taken seriously and trusted (Monaghan, 2018). CSR has taken on a much larger, more global meaning that pushes the concept of local, nationalistic cultural respect.

We live in a world where consumers want to spend their money with socially aware and active corporations and where consumers are looking for their social values to be mirrored in the companies they support (Monaghan, 2018; Prezly, 2019). What could easily be communicated to one region's consumers and left unknown to another is beginning to blur as social media continues to connect us. Multinational corporations may find that they can no longer have their cake and eat it too in each regional market as what they communicate in one may have consequences in another.

While Blizzard is a company that in some degree does support its LGBTQ community and wants to help make the gaming and esports culture, and society at large, more accepting of LGBTQ, their mission of diversity appears to prioritize nationalistic cultural identities due to feared backlash from fans, corporate, and government partners who do not value or approve of LGBTQ rights. Blizzard must decide if a focus on diversity is only a side note strategy or they must come out loud and proud.

Notes

1 https://twitter.com/westofhouse/status/812110259737137152?lang=en
2 https://twitter.com/playoverwatch/status/811276193207111680?lang=en
3 https://twitter.com/PlayOverwatch/status/1082351191072202753?s=20
4 https://twitter.com/westofhouse/status/1082394625837428736?lang=en
5 https://overwatchleague.com/en-us/about
6 https://rlewisreports.com/wp-content/uploads/2018/03/OWLRulebook.pdf
7 https://overwatchleague.com/en-gb/news/21834451/celebrate-pride-with-the-overwatch-league
8 https://overwatchleague.com/en-us/news/23013827/show-your-pride
9 https://twitter.com/overwatchleague/status/1136407349608902658?s=11
10 https://twitter.com/Blizzard_Ent/status/1134509599208484864/photo/1
11 www.instagram.com/p/ByIpGZnjOjv/?igshid=ghp3ggr6hzlz
12 Full disclosure: I am a member of QWEERTY Gamers and joined them for the Pride 2019 event.
13 This writer viewed from the U.S.
14 https://twitter.com/overwatchleague/status/1137122059774042112
15 https://twitter.com/overwatchleague/status/1137236378075521024
16 www.instagram.com/p/BycCCrMAmGF/?igshid=1ccua6o9wn2or
17 https://twitter.com/search?f=live&pf=on&q=kit%20kat%20rivalry%20(from%3Aoverwatchleague)&src=typed_query
18 https://twitter.com/lagladiators/status/1136027402906193920

References

Bell, B. C. (2019, June 14). *Overwatch League's Pride Day censored in South Korea*. Retrieved June 14, 2019 from www.outsports.com/2019/6/14/18677940/esports-overwatch-league-pride-day-south-korea

Bortree, D., & Haigh, M. (2018, May). International CSR: Challenges of implementing corporate responsibility programs across the globe. *Public Relations Journal*, *11*(4), special issue: *International CSR*. Retrieved July 29, 2019 from https://prjournal.instituteforpr.org/wp-content/uploads/Bortree-Haigh-intro-final-1.pdf.

Campbell, C. (2017, March 20). *Overwatch's search for diversity*. Retrieved from www.polygon.com/features/2017/3/20/14960924/overwatch-diversity-jeff-kaplan-interview-blizzard/comment/420505895

Castells, M. (2012). *Networks of outrage and hope: Social movements in the internet age*. Cambridge: Polity Press.

D'Anastasio, C. (2019, June 10). *South Korean Overwatch League broadcast apparently omits Pride Day festivities*. Retrieved June 14, 2019 from https://kotaku.com/south-korean-overwatch-league-broadcast-apparently-omit-1835379449

Gough, C. (2019, July 25). *Overwatch player count worldwide 2018*. Retrieved July 28, 2019 from www.statista.com/statistics/618035/number-gamers-overwatch-worldwide/

Griffiths, J. (2019, April 17). *Can you be gay online in China? Social media companies aren't sure*. Retrieved July 28, 2019 from www.cnn.com/2019/04/17/tech/weibo-china-censorship-lgbt-intl/index.html

Hung-Baesecke, C., Chen, Y. R., Stacks, D., Coombs, W., & Boyd, B. (2018, May). Creating shared value, public trust, supportive behavior, and communication preferences: A comparison study in the United States and China. *Public Relations Journal, 11*(4), special issue: *International CSR*, 1–21. Retrieved July 29, 2019 from https://prjournal.instituteforpr.org/wp-content/uploads/Flora-Final.pdf

Joseph, M. (2019, June 21). *Opinion | As more companies wade in, it's time to ask: Is pride for sale?* Retrieved July 28, 2019 from www.washingtonpost.com/graphics/2019/opinions/pride-for-sale/?noredirect=on&utm_term=.fc33c498062b

Kim, S., & Ferguson, M. T. (2014). Public expectations of CSR communication: What and how to communicate CSR. *Public Relations Journal, 8*, 1–22. Retrieved July 27, 2019 from https://bellisario.psu.edu/assets/uploads/2014KIMFERGUSON.pdf

Monaghan, B. (2018, February 13). *PR for a purpose: Bringing corporate social responsibility back to basics*. Retrieved July 28, 2019 from www.forbes.com/sites/forbesagencycouncil/2018/02/13/pr-for-a-purpose-bringing-corporate-social-responsibility-back-to-basics/

News. (2018, June 1). *Los Angeles Valiant establish unprecedented partnership with you can play project*. Retrieved from https://valiant.overwatchleague.com/en-us/news/los-angeles-valiant-establish-unprecedented-partnership-you-can-play-project

Newsbeat, B. (2016, December 21). *Russia blocks Overwatch comic over gay character: BBC newsbeat*. Retrieved from www.bbc.co.uk/newsbeat/article/38391018/russia-blocks-overwatch-comic-over-gay-character

Oh, A. (2019, January 7). *Blizzard quietly confirms another LGBTQ Overwatch hero*. Retrieved January 7, 2019 from www.polygon.com/2019/1/7/18172470/overwatch-soldier-76-gay-bisexual

Prezly. (2019, April 5). *The relationship between PR and CSR: Prezly*. Retrieved July 28, 2019 from www.prezly.com/academy/relationships/corporate-social-responsibility/the-relationship-between-pr-and-csr

Reeves, H. (2016). Defining public relations' role in corporate social responsibility programs. *PR Journal, 10*(2), Summer/Fall, 1–19. Retrieved July 29, 2019 from https://prjournal.instituteforpr.org/wp-content/uploads/reeves_nz3.pdf

Rossi, M. (2015, November 7). *Overwatch will be diverse, include gay characters*. Retrieved from https://blizzardwatch.com/2015/11/07/overwatch-will-diverse-include-gay-characters/

Savery, A. (2019, June 7). *What pride means to a cyberpunk shieldmaiden*. Retrieved June 7, 2019 from https://overwatchleague.com/en-us/news/23013834/what-pride-means-to-a-cyberpunk-shieldmaiden

Serrao, N. (2016, December 21). *"Overwatch" comic confirms key character is a lesbian.* Retrieved from https://ew.com/gaming/2016/12/21/overwatch-tracer-confirmed-lesbian/

Valens, A. (2019, January 8). *Soldier: 76 is Overwatch's next queer hero-but fans want more.* Retrieved January 8, 2019 from www.dailydot.com/parsec/overwatch-soldier-76-queer-hero/

White, C. & Fitzpatrick, K. (2018). Corporate Perspectives on the Role of Global Public Relations in Public Diplomacy. *Public Relations Journal*, 11(4).

8 Engaging audiences with authenticity

The role of social media in Royal Caribbean's hurricane relief effort

Jessalynn Strauss and Kathleen Stansberry

Background: a growing company, a growing sector in the tourism industry

One of the newest and fastest-growing sectors of the tourism economy, cruise travel has come increasingly into focus as the number of cruisers grows every year. In its annual "state of the industry" report, Cruise Lines International Association (CLIA), the industry's professional body, estimated that almost 30 million people around the globe would take a cruise in 2019 (CLIA, 2018). That organization has estimated the global economic impact of the cruise industry at $134 billion, with over a million full-time jobs created by the industry.

After a spate of mergers and acquisitions in the late 1980s and 1990s, the now-highly concentrated cruise industry has three corporations (Carnival, Royal Caribbean, and Norwegian) that account for over 75% of cruise revenue (Clancy, 2017). The Royal Caribbean Cruises, Ltd. corporation owns and operates six cruise lines, including Royal Caribbean International (RCI) as well as Celebrity Cruises, German-based TUI Cruises, Spanish-speaking Pullmantur Cruises, boutique cruise line Azamara Club Cruises, and luxury operator Silversea Cruises (Royal Caribbean Intl., 2019).

The Caribbean islands, located to the south of the eastern half of the continental United States and stretching down toward South America, have played a pivotal role in the development of the modern cruise industry (Clancy, 2017). The proximity of these islands to the mainland U.S. made them attractive locales for early leisure cruises, which made their departures from South Florida. About one in three cruises goes to the Caribbean islands (Clancy, 2017).

Situation: devastating storms make landfall in the Caribbean

On August 31, 2017, Hurricane Irma developed in the Atlantic Ocean. Within a few days, fueled by warm ocean waters, Irma developed into one

DOI: 10.4324/9780429327094-9

of the most powerful Category 5 hurricanes on record. Irma made land-fall on September 5, slamming into several northeastern Caribbean islands (Rivera & Alvarez, 2017).

As Irma approached Florida on an unpredictable path, Royal Caribbean cancelled a number of cruises leaving from the state's many ports. The company repurposed those cruise ship resources to move a number of Royal Caribbean employees out of the path of the storm, leaving a skeleton crew at the company's headquarters in South Florida (Lui, 2017). The company's CEO and high-level managers, along with communications officers, combined to form a dynamic crisis response team on board the *Enchantment of the Seas*, a ship whose sailing had been cancelled due to the storm (Personal Interview, 2017).

Royal Caribbean also pressed its vessels into service to deliver relief supplies to the islands that had already been affected by Irma. The *Majesty of the Seas* was dispatched to carry food, water, and medical supplies to St. Thomas and St. Maarten, two of the hardest-hit islands, and to bring displaced tourists back to Puerto Rico, which had been largely spared by Irma (Wyss, 2017).

Less than two weeks after Hurricane Irma made landfall, Hurricane Maria roared through the already battered Caribbean islands. Maria devastated the island of Puerto Rico, a home port for Royal Caribbean, knocking out all power to the island. Royal Caribbean responded by cancelling the sailing of *Adventure of the Seas* on September 30 in order to use the ship to provide further humanitarian relief. During its week-long mission, *Adventure* delivered supplies to hard-hit areas such as St. Maarten and evacuated Puerto Ricans (Herrera, 2017).

Royal Caribbean's relief efforts following Hurricanes Irma and Maria were significant. By its own account, the cruise line delivered over 30,000 gallons of water, more than 25 pallets of medical supplies, and 450 generators along with evacuating over 5500 people (Royal Caribbean Intl., 2017). "We were doing what we were doing because it was the right thing to do. And frankly, we were all really busy, and not so much thinking about the PR-ability of everything," Royal Caribbean's lead content strategist for social media Nathalie Fernandez said (Personal interview, 2017).

Although the intent behind Royal Caribbean's relief efforts was humanitarian, by showcasing those works through social media in near real time, the company garnered support from its existing audience and earned widespread media coverage. An established social media presence with team members in constant contact with senior management helped fuel the success of Royal Caribbean's communication efforts.

Communicating the response: social media steps in

Royal Caribbean's social media efforts are overseen by a multifaceted team responsible for planning, creation, and distribution of content across multiple platforms. Team members track the success of engagement for each social media post and often adjust their plans accordingly (Personal interview, 2017). The social media team's ability to be nimble and flexible, along with its dedication to constantly preparing and practicing its crisis communication plans, enabled the organization to leverage established online relationships with customers and fans in the aftermath of Hurricanes Irma and Maria.

During the hurricane crisis, social media initially served as a valuable tool for Royal Caribbean to communicate with its guests, many of whom had questions about their upcoming cruise sailings. The team works with a number of call-center employees to aim for a response time around 12 minutes for customer questions asked on social media (Personal interview, 2017). An uptick in the number of questions, along with internal alerts, led the team to realize in early September 2017 that the oncoming Hurricane Irma would put the previously established crisis plans to the test.

Several members of Royal Caribbean's social media team were part of a core group of organizational leaders who relocated to one of the company's cruise ships. The physical proximity of the communications team, which was on board the ship with CEO and top management, allowed for constant assessment of existing communication efforts and adaptation as needed. The presence of the communications team also ensured that communications remained a focus of the corporation's larger crisis response.

Although the purpose of Royal Caribbean's relief efforts were humanitarian rather than strategic, the communications team quickly realized that it should communicate with stakeholders about these efforts. "We are a very large company that frequents the Caribbean often, and I feel like personally when things like this happen, you want to know what the big companies are doing," said Kristin Perera, senior community strategist for social media at Royal Caribbean (Personal interview, 2017).

In many cases, Royal Caribbean's ships – and their continued connection to power and the Internet – were the only source of communication from islands whose infrastructure had been demolished by the hurricanes. As a result, many of the early reports of damage from these islands came from Royal Caribbean or its partners as they brought supplies and evacuated stranded tourists on islands like St. Maarten and Puerto Rico.

The team decided on two primary goals for social media engagement after the hurricanes: informing stakeholders of the company's efforts and attempting to engage them in the relief efforts (Personal interview, 2017). Posts showcasing relief efforts on Royal Caribbean's Facebook and Instagram accounts featured candid photos of crew members unloading supplies; others showed entire families being evacuated on Royal Caribbean ships. These shots stood in stark contrast to the highly stylized images of lush tropical landscapes and extravagant ship amenities that normally dominate cruise industry postings.

The communications team made transparency a focus of its strategy and provided frequent updates about the company's efforts. Employees talked about the company's relief operation as a sort of moral imperative; as community strategist Perera said, "It's one thing for a company to say we care about the Caribbean, but I think it's another to actually do something about [it]" (Personal interview, 2017). According to Celia De La Llama, corporate communications consultant for Royal Caribbean, social media was used as a tool to help continue the focus on hurricane relief efforts for a longer period of time:

> I think it's so easy with the news cycle for . . . certain things to be forgotten very quickly, and one of the ways I felt that [Royal Caribbean] combatted that was to just continue sharing information about those Caribbean islands and . . . sharing the stories of the people who actually lived there, so people wouldn't forget, people would continue to help.

The team focused on Facebook, which its members felt best reflected the demographic of the cruise line's guests, as the primary tool for engagement. Messages were pushed to other social media platforms, including Instagram and Twitter, and the company's usual glossy photos of tropical destinations were joined by action shots of crew members unloading pallets of water in the hot Caribbean sun. The relief photos weren't nearly as polished as the company's preplanned glamour shots of its destinations, but their authenticity must have struck a chord, because messages focused on relief efforts generated far more engagement than others. These social media posts were often followed by a spike in donations to aid the company's relief efforts (Personal interview, 2017).

Royal Caribbean's strong social media presence in the wake of the hurricanes also generated positive coverage in both trade and mainstream media. As content strategist Fernandez recounted:

> Social led to trade media starting to ask questions, and emailing us for information, for which we made [Royal Caribbean CEO] Michael Bayley available, which then led to mainstream media and a segment on GMA on Monday morning from the ship in the middle of the ocean with Michael. So I think part of what the social channels did was obviously communicating with our guests, but just providing news updates as well, which then led to mainstream media coverage.

The company's relief efforts were featured positively in national publications such as *USA Today*, CNBC, and *Fortune* as well as local outlets, including the *Miami Herald* and the *New York Daily News*.

Lessons learned: the (unexpected) value of social media in a crisis

Royal Caribbean's quick-thinking communication about its hurricane relief efforts in September 2017 shows not only the necessity for a corporation to include real-time communication in its crisis response strategies but also the number of ways in which effective social media communication can benefit a company's communications on other platforms.

Social media has obviously proven to be an effective tool for customer relations, and Royal Caribbean's experience during the hurricanes showed this to be even more true in crisis situations. The company was receiving queries from guests faster than it could respond to them – in an interview, one employee suggested that a larger response team would be used in the future in order to enhance the company's bandwidth for responding to customers. These efforts were rewarded by an effective and surprisingly wide-ranging distribution of pertinent information to customers: In some cases, cruise guests were learning about developments in Royal Caribbean's response from social media before hearing from their own travel agents. The shareability of social media made these platforms effective in disseminating information widely.

Messaging on social media also helped propel the company toward positive coverage in traditional media. Approached first by trade publications, Royal Caribbean responded quickly to these queries, making its CEO available to talk about relief efforts and the company's overall response to the hurricanes. As a result, the story gained traction and made the leap to popular outlets such as *USA Today* and *Good Morning America*, providing a great deal more visibility for the company's relief efforts.

Finally, the personal nature of social media allowed Royal Caribbean to portray its relief efforts in a much more human way, providing an authenticity that resonated with the company's stakeholders. Through emotional pictures such as family reunions and rescued pets, Royal Caribbean told a story of disaster response that resonated with many people, as shown by the unusually high engagement generated by these social media messages.

While strategic planning is always a key component of successful crisis communications, this example of Royal Caribbean's success in distributing pictures of its relief efforts via social media shows that it's equally important to be flexible when new opportunities arise. By communicating the company's actions in real time, Royal Caribbean was able to keep stakeholders engaged in hurricane relief efforts long beyond the traditional news cycle.

Using pictures of workers delivering supplies and families being rescued from ravaged islands, Royal Caribbean was able to effectively engage its audience on social media. These audiences became involved themselves by sharing information or donating to the company's relief efforts. By facilitating stakeholder promotion of its socially responsible efforts, Royal Caribbean attained a rare achievement: communication that was both authentic and positively received by audiences.

References

Clancy, M. (2017). Power and profits in the global cruise industry. In *Cruise ship tourism* (pp. 43–56). Oxfordshire: CABI.

CLIA (Cruise Lines International Association). (2018). *2019 cruise industry outlook*. Retrieved August 5, 2019 from www.cruising.org/news-and-research/research/2018/december/2019-state-of-the-industry

Herrera, C. (2017, October 3). Cruise ship carries thousands of hurricane evacuees to Fort Lauderdale. *Miami Herald*. Retrieved from www.miamiherald.com/

Lui, K. (2017, September 8). Hurricane Irma: Royal Caribbean uses cruise ship to evacuate employees. *Fortune*. Retrieved from http://fortune.com/

Personal Interview. (2017, October 27). Conducted with Royal Caribbean cruise lines employees Nathalie Fernandez (Lead Content Strategist, Social Media); Kristin Perera (Senior Community Strategist, Social Media), and Celia De La Llama (Consultant, Corporate Communications).

Rivera, I., & Alvarez, L. (2017, September 5). Hurricane Irma, packing 185-M.P.H. winds, makes landfall in Caribbean. *The New York Times*. Retrieved from www.nytimes.com/

Royal Caribbean Intl. (2017). Updates | *Hurricane disaster relief*. Retrieved November 1, 2017 from www.royalcaribbean.com/cruise-ships/hurricane-disaster-relief

Royal Caribbean Intl. (2019). *About Royal Caribbean cruises, ltd*. Retrieved August 5, 2019 from www.rclcorporate.com/about/

Wyss, J. (2017, September 18). They booked a 5-day pleasure cruise: They wound up on a 2-week hurricane relief mission. *Miami Herald*. Retrieved from www.miamiherald.com/

9 A virus and viral content

The Vietnam government's use of TikTok for public health messages during the COVID-19 pandemic

Kylie P. Torres

Introduction

During the 2020 COVID-19 global pandemic, government organizations used a variety of public relations tactics to communicate messages about handwashing, social distancing, and other public health measures to stop the spread of the virus. In addition to proven social media platforms like Facebook and YouTube, the Vietnamese government helped produce a TikTok video with information on how to stop the spread of the virus. The video amassed 40 million views, leading more organizations to consider the value of TikTok, especially in reaching younger demographics. This case study will examine Vietnam's use of TikTok as a tool to spread health messages during the COVID-19 pandemic, the Structural Virality of Online Diffusion, and why this is important for public relations strategies.

TikTok

TikTok, established in 2016, is a social media platform designed to share user-generated content ("About: TikTok-Real Short Videos," n.d.). At the time of the 2020 COVID-19 global pandemic, TikTok was the leading platform for short videos recorded using a mobile phone ("Most Popular Social Media Platforms" 2020). While the videos range in content and format, the most popular TikTok videos are vlogs (video diaries), lip-sync videos, and user-created dances ("What Is TikTok?" 2020). The application has approximately 800 million users who spend an average of 45 minutes a day on the application ("Most Popular Social Media Platforms," 2020; Iqbal, 2020).

Although most creators of TikTok content are general users, the application is growing in popularity with brands and organizations like Disney and the NBA (Gravante, 2020; Bump, 2019). Across Asia just over one-third of social media users have a TikTok account, this is the most dense number of TikTok users in the world (Iqbal, 2020). In Vietnam alone, the country

DOI: 10.4324/9780429327094-10

has 12 million individual users and the highest growth of consumers in Southeast Asia (Yinglun, 2020). Globally, 41% of TikTok users are between the ages of 16 and 24 and 50% are under the age of 34 (Aslam, 2020). Sixty-eight percent of users just look at content on the application and do not generate any of their own content, while 55% of users do generate original content (Aslam, 2020).

Social media content and virility

"Viral" is a term used to describe a social media post or content that appears to organically spread among users, generating thousands or millions of views, likes, comments, or other interactions (Peterson, 2014). While this may appear to mimic the viral spread of a "microscopic organism" and some social media posts have indeed seen widespread sharing without promotion or commercial intervention, public relations and marketing professionals employ paid optimization and other techniques to increase the visibility of their posts – organic success is extremely uncommon.

When social media spreads far from its source, this means it has gone viral (Peterson, 2014). Viral posts happen when content is shared multiple times, not just viewed multiple times (Peterson, 2014). For example, if a YouTube video has one million views, it has not gone viral. If the same video has one million shares, it has gone viral. This means individual users are sharing the content and making it spread, versus it just staying in one place online. Social media posts can be spread by sharing them on Facebook, via messenger platforms, or even re-shared on the same platform they were originally posted on.

A brand or organization wants their social media content to go viral in order to increase visibility of their subject matter (D'Ottavio, 2020). Having a post go viral is comparable to word of mouth advertising, it gets the content to many audience members through virility and it is overall low cost (D'Ottavio, 2020). Viral content is also known to increase individual users' interaction with the post in the form of comments, discussions, and reactions. All of this is considerable for brand visibility (D'Ottavio, 2020).

Social media use in the 2020 COVID-19 pandemic

COVID-19 is an infectious virus that was discovered in 2019. The illness was first found in China and quickly dispersed, leading to a global pandemic. ("About Covid-19" n.d.). As of October 2020 there had been 39,415,643 recorded cases and 1,105,621 recorded deaths worldwide (Tracking Covid-19's global spread, n.d.).

The pandemic resulted in a mandatory quarantine in many countries worldwide (De Valck, 2020). As a result, social media became a "lifeline" for many during quarantine (De Valck, 2020). Caregivers of young children, particularly mothers, turned to social media for support during times of homeschooling and lockdown. Caregivers expressed feelings of helplessness and depression with the extra burden, so they turned to humor on social media (Lemish & Elias, 2020). On a global scale, users turned to social media to find news, public health information, and human connection during the COVID-19 pandemic (Pfefferbaum & North, 2021).

Worldwide, no one has been untouched by the social effects of the virus (Pfefferbaum & North, 2021). Individuals have experienced feelings of insecurity, emotional isolation, as well as confusion (Pfefferbaum & North, 2021). A poll taken in the United States during March 2020 showed that 32% of adults reported their mental health had been negatively impacted by the social effects of COVID-19 and by mid-July 2020 that number increased to 53% (Panchal et al., 2020). Another poll was conducted during March and May of 2020 that showed about 50% of adults in the United States had increased their social media use since lockdowns began, and 60% of these adults were aged 18 to 34 (Samet, 2020). In teens aged 13 to 17, polls have found there has been an increased social media use of 63% in the United States (Mendoza, 2020).

The TikTok application saw a usage increase of 75% from January 2020 to September of the same year (Koetsier, 2020). This means they have 33 times more users than the nearest competing company, a similar application called Likee (Koetsier, 2020). The continued growth of TikTok during the pandemic, especially during lockdown periods when social media growth increased in usage overall, suggests opportunities for the platform to be used for broader public relations and communication efforts, beyond entertainment and personal usage.

"Viral" public health messages on TikTok in Vietnam

While social media has been widely adopted by government organizations to communicate public health messages, the COVID-19 pandemic provided one of the first opportunities to include TikTok in such efforts. In the early months of the lockdown, many influencers and individual users created informative and entertaining videos to share proper handwashing instructions, often using popular songs or writing their own songs to make messages more entertaining and to appeal to younger demographics (McCarthy, 2020).

In addition to country-wide text messages about COVID-19 safety and informational posters, the Vietnam government created the #EndCoV project (Jones, 2020; Hoang, 2020). This public relations campaign included a song called "Ghen Cô Vy," a cartoon, and a handwashing dance challenge on social media (Hoang, 2020). The lyrics to the song were written by two popular Vietnamese lyricists, it was sung by VPop stars MIN and Erik, and the choreographed dance challenge was created by the celebrity Quang Đăng (Hoang, 2020). The song, cartoon, and dance were all produced by Vietnam's National Institute of Occupational Health and Environment (NIOEH) and encouraged COVID-19 safe practices, such as proper handwashing and social distancing (Hoang, 2020). The goal of the campaign was to get out the message that "prevention is better than a cure" and to join the community together to build good habits (Hoang, 2020). This campaign gained support from the United Nation Development Program and UNICEF (Hoang, 2020).

For their campaign, NIOEH first worked with artists to create the song and then released it on Quang Đăng's personal TikTok page as a dance challenge in February 2020. The challenge called for users to tag two friends in the comments and for these friends to make their own version of the video on TikTok (Mamo, 2020). This challenge was widespread and even reached out to users in remote Vietnamese villages (Pti, 2020). Participants also included users with verified accounts, adding to the popularity of the challenge, including one from UNICEF's official TikTok account (Eghtesadi & Florea, 2020). Between February and October 2020, the challenge had over 40 million views and almost 85 thousand unique user-generated videos. The month following the dance challenge's debut NIOEH released the song again accompanied by a fun cartoon on YouTube through VPop star MIN's personal YouTube channel.

Structural virility of diffusion and public health messages on TikTok

Based on the concept of Diffusion Theory, Goel, Anderson, Hofman, and Watts have developed a formula for the Structural Virality of Online Diffusion (2015). Based on their studies, they concluded that the average size of a diffusion tree is 1.3. This means that for every 10 posts of content there are, on average, three additional downstream adoptions appearing through sharing of content.

The Structural Virality of Online Diffusion differs from standard media diffusion by the way it spreads. Standard media, such as television, is one source that is spread out directly to individual consumers (Goel, Anderson, Hofman, & Watts, 2015). Online Diffusion spreads more like a tree grows. In Online Diffusion, the trunk of the tree is the original social media post (Goel, Anderson, Hofman, & Watts, 2015). The different large segments coming off the tree's main trunk is like when individuals share a post on social media, it splits to different viewers. Then, those branches split off again, and again, until it eventually ends. This is how Structural Virality of Online Diffusion is unique compared to more traditional platforms. Viral Diffusion shows how social media applications like TikTok spread content. Instead of one large broadcast that many individuals all consume at one time, like a radio broadcast, the content on TikTok is shared, dueted, and spread through more of a growing branch than a direct line.

Vietnam's dance challenge successfully branched off and spread via TikTok. Because the challenge called for users to tag two friends in the comments and to challenge those friends to remake the video themselves, the tree trunk that was celebrity Đăng's first video was able to spread into many branches. This is how the song was able to generate about 85 thousand unique videos uploaded by individual users, all over Vietnam, and beyond. These videos spread out like a tree in all directions. By the Vietnamese government using their resources, understanding their audience, and creating a fun song about COVID-19 safety, they were able to create a seed for the viral tree.

This content going viral benefited Vietnam by getting credible information out to many of its citizens. TikTok is known to be used by a younger audience and two-thirds of Vietnam's 97 million citizens are under the age of 35 (Pti, 2020). For physicians in Vietnam that were working in youth clinics, the popular song created a commonality that they could use to discuss proper handwashing and ways of preventing COVID-19. This TikTok trend became a powerful tool to help doctors enforce factual and accurate medical advice (Eghtesadi & Florea, 2020).

Another way it has benefited Vietnam is through combating misinformation. Viral content can exacerbate misinformation; however, with the right research beforehand and an understanding on how to get verified information out into the public, it can be a great tool. Many countries could use Vietnam's case as a model to create their own viral communication about how to stay safe during the COVID-19 pandemic.

Vietnam's quick response to COVID-19 was successful (Jones, 2020). The country's first recorded case of the virus was on January 23, 2020 and by the next month the #EndCoV campaign was already fully launched (Jones, 2020). Vietnam put out information and implemented policies regarding the virus that took other countries months to compile and enforce (Jones, 2020). Because of the quick action and clear communication messages, Vietnam has had less than 1,500 cases of COVID as of December 2020 and 35 deaths, which is shockingly low for a population of 97 million (Jones, 2020).

Conclusion

As of March 2020, only 4% of social media marketers were using TikTok (Vela, 2020). Public relations professionals need to be sure they are not discounting emerging platforms, like TikTok, in their campaigns. It is the quickest growing application currently, worldwide, which means it's an excellent platform for opportunity. Since 2018 Americans have spent over 23 million dollars on TikTok in-app purchases (Vela, 2020).

TikTok is known as an "Anti-Marketing" platform. This is because Tik-Tokers are not digesting an average campaign. Users on this platform are used to seeing videos that feature influencers, incorporate a fun song with a dance, or perhaps tell a joke. The application is full of trends that public relations and marketing professionals can keep up and incorporate in their campaigns, this is known as trendjacking (Vela, 2020). These video campaigns are low budget and should be made to look like they are created by at home amateurs (Vela, 2020). They are meant to be simple, engaging, and positive.

Using social media to communicate to the public is essential and it creates impactful messaging that can reach a large audience quickly. The best way for public relations professionals to get their messages out through social media is for them to post often, post quality content, and to understand how the information spreads. By coupling this with a celebrity and a fun song, Vietnam's campaign can be used as an example of how to help push content toward going viral, particularly now during a pandemic, when all eyes are on social media.

References

About Covid-19. (n.d.). Retrieved from https://www.cdc.gov/coronavirus/2019-ncov/cdcresponse/about-COVID-19.html

About: TikTok-Real Short Videos. (n.d.). Retrieved September 1, 2020 from www.tiktok.com/about?lang=en

Aslam, S. (2020, October 28). *TikTok by the numbers: Stats, femographics & gun facts.* Retrieved December 30, 2020 from www.omnicoreagency.com/tiktok-statistics/#:~:text=41%20percent%20of%20TikTok%20users,26%25%20between%2018%20and%2024

Bump, P. (2019, September 9). *How 7 brands are using TikTok.* Retrieved December 30, 2020 from https://blog.hubspot.com/marketing/brands-on-tiktok

De Valck, K. (2020, April 7). *What is the role of social media during the COVID-19 crisis?* Retrieved December 15, 2020 from www.hec.edu/en/knowledge/instants/what-role-social-media-during-covid-19-crisis-0

D'Ottavio, D. (2020, March 20). *Social media's role in viral content marketing.* Retrieved December 30, 2020 from https://blog.frac.tl/social-media-viral-marketing

Eghtesadi, M., & Florea, A. (2020, June). Facebook, Instagram, Reddit and TikTok: A proposal for health authorities to integrate popular social media platforms in contingency planning amid a global pandemic outbreak. *Canadian Journal of*

Public Health = *Revue Canadienne de Sante Publique, 111*(3), 389–391. https://doi.org/10.17269/s41997-020-00343-0

Goel, S., Anderson, A., Hofman, J., & Watts, D. J. (2015). The structural virality of online diffusion. *Management Science.* 150722112809007. doi:10.1287/mnsc.2015.2158

Gravante, A. (2020, October 22). *Experience disney magic in whole new way with @DisneyParks on TikTok.* Retrieved December 30, 2020 from https://disneyparks.disney.go.com/blog/2020/10/experience-disney-magic-in-whole-new-way-with-disneyparks-on-tiktok/

Hoang, H. (2020, October 4). *Ghen Co Vy official English nersion coronavirus song together we #EndCoV.* Retrieved December 30, 2020 from http://nioeh.org.vn/tin-tuc/ghen-co-vy-official-english-version-%7C-coronavirus-song-%7C-together-we-endcov

Iqbal, M. (2020, June 23). *TikTok revenue and usage statistics (2020).* Retrieved August 1, 2020 from www.businessofapps.com/data/tik-tok-statistics/

Jones, A. (2020, May 15). *Coronavirus: How "overreaction" made Vietnam a virus success.* Retrieved December 30, 2020 from www.bbc.com/news/world-asia-52628283

Koetsier, J. (2020, September 15). *Massive TikTok growth: Up 75% this year, now 33X more users than nearest direct competitor.* Retrieved December 15, 2020 from www.forbes.com/sites/johnkoetsier/2020/09/14/massive-tiktok-growth-up-75-this-year-now-33x-more-users-than-nearest-competitor/?sh=781032704fe4

Lemish, D., & Elias, N. (2020). "We decided we don't want children: We will let them know tonight": Parental humor on social media in a time of coronavirus pandemic. *International Journal of Communication (Online),* 5261.

Panchal, N., Kamal, R., Orgera, K., Cox, C., Garfield, R., Hamel, L.,…Chidambaram, P. (2020, August 21). *The implications of COVID-19 for mental health and substance use.* Retrieved December 30, 2020 from www.kff.org/coronavirus-covid-19/issue-brief/the-implications-of-covid-19-for-mental-health-and-substance-use/

Peterson, J. (2014, October 14). *How defining virality reveals the truth about viral content.* Retrieved September 1, 2020 from www.scripted.com/content-marketing/viral-content-definition

Pfefferbaum, B., North, C., & Others. (2021, May 5). Mental health and the covid-19 pandemic: Nejm. Retrieved from https://www.nejm.org/doi/full/10.1056/nejmp2008017

Pti. (2020, March 4). *Vietnam handwash dance challenge: Take a break from coronavirus panic: Vietnam's handwash dance challenge goes viral.* Retrieved September 11, 2020 from https://economictimes.indiatimes.com/magazines/panache/take-a-break-from-coronavirus-panic-vietnams-handwash-dance-challenge-goes-viral/articleshow/74457876.cms

Mamo, H. (2020, March 9). *Vietnam's viral coronavirus PSA sparked a TikTok dance challenge & these are 10 of the best videos.* Retrieved August 1, 2020 from www.billboard.com/articles/news/international/9329174/vietnam-coronavirus-psa-song-best-tiktok-dance-videos

McCarthy, K. (2020, March 6). *How parents can navigate coronavirus news on social media with their kids*. Retrieved December 31, 2020 from www.goodmornin gamerica.com/family/story/talk-kids-viral-tiktok-coronavirus-videos-69431277

Mendoza, N. (2020, September 7). *63% of parents say teens' social media use has increased during COVID-19*. Retrieved December 30, 2020 from www.techre public.com/article/63-of-parents-say-teens-social-media-use-has-increased-dur ing-covid-19/

Most Popular Social Media Platforms. (2020, April). Retrieved September 1, 2020 from www.oberlo.com/statistics/most-popular-social-media-platforms

Samet, A. (2020, July 29). *How the coronavirus is changing US social media usage*. Retrieved December 30, 2020 from www.emarketer.com/content/how-corona virus-changing-us-social-media-usage

Tracking Covid-19's global spread. (n.d.). Retrieved from https://www.cnn.com/ interactive/2020/health/coronavirus-maps-and-cases/

Vela, G. (2020, March 19). *Council post: TikTok: The next frontier of social media is here*. Retrieved December 30, 2020 from www.forbes.com/sites/forbesagency council/2020/03/19/tiktok-the-next-frontier-of-social-media-is-here/?sh= 18ad1dac2426

What Is TikTok? (2020, October 26). Retrieved December 20, 2020 from https:// influencermarketinghub.com/what-is-tiktok/

Yinglun, S. (Ed.). (2020, September 20). *Vietnam, TikTok join hands for bet ter child protection*. Retrieved December 15, 2020 from www.xinhuanet.com/ english/2019-09/20/c_138408459.htm

Index

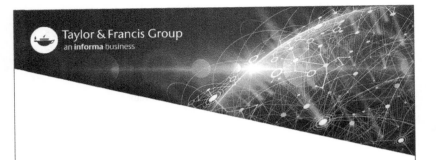

For Product Safety Concerns and Information please contact our EU
representative GPSR@taylorandfrancis.com Taylor & Francis Verlag GmbH,
Kaufingerstraße 24, 80331 München, Germany

Printed and bound by CPI Group (UK) Ltd, Croydon, CR0 4YY

08/06/2025

01897001-0006